Praise for

PLEASE WAIT BY THE COATROOM

"Over the twenty-five years that I have been a museum curator, I have turned to John Yau's writing about the aesthetics of exclusion and fundamentals on how to operate as an Asian American *in* the art world, though we have been made to feel we are not *of* or *from* it. Yau writes with grace, complexity, and deep exploration."

—CHRISTINE Y. KIM
Britton Family Curator-at-Large, North America Art, Tate Modern

"John Yau's insight into the work of artists who refuse to adhere to corporate and collector interests is unparalleled. His clear prose and intellectual curiosity come through on every page as he challenges us to think about art independent of lazy art-market narratives. For John, art is life."

—HRAG VARTANIAN
Editor-in-chief and co-founder of Hyperallergic

"John Yau's criticism illuminates artists as makers, thinkers, and perhaps most radically, as people. He demonstrates the power of looking for yourself and saying what you mean, and challenges all of us do the same."

—MARCI KWON
Co-Director, Asian American Art Initiative, Cantor Arts Center

"Poet and critic John Yau offers an intellectually lush collection of essays redefining the quest for identity with nuance, humor, and grace. There is nothing myopic or didactic here; Yau tells the story of excellence, precarity, and unsung heroes of painting, sculpture, and photography who continue to navigate the bowels of inequity. Yau's description of seeing Wifredo Lam's painting hanging in the hallway to the coatroom at the Museum of Modern art will go down in history as the quintessential example of the experience of thousands of artists of color lucky enough to be collected. He deftly uses this opportunity to excavate a generation of inequality in the global art worlds, but particularly in New York."

—KIM ANNO
Painter, photographer, and film/video artist

"John Yau's *Please Wait by the Coatroom* is the latest entry into the august tradition of poets writing about art."

—HELEN MOLESWORTH
Writer and curator

"John Yau's art criticism is luscious and purposeful. He is generous with words, but not in an adulatory way. Rather, Yau aims at sounding the dimensions of an artist's oeuvre and at unlocking its hermeneutic potential. This collection, which bears the name of his landmark 1988 essay on Wifredo Lam's marginalization at MoMA, gathers his voluminous work on artists of a wide variety of ethnic and cultural backgrounds, recognizing the importance of personal identity as a defining element of artistic expression. The collection is restitutive of what the art mainstream and formalist frameworks have tried to erase. Yau illuminates a world of artists disregarded or omitted in the modern art canon. Giving them the attention they deserve, this book is a breath of fresh air, and evidence of Yau's lifetime of swimming against the mainstream's conventions and hierarchies."

—TAÍNA CARAGOL
Curator of painting, sculpture & Latinx art and history, National Portrait Gallery, Smithsonian

"John Yau's radiance of words and glistening observations about artists and the cultural sphere inspire and provoke. His peerless mode of describing and insights into the feeling of being cast aside compels all of us to reconsider makers and histories that have been waiting to be seen. Another brave, finely wrought collection that I will dip into time and time again."

—ASMA NAEEM
Dorothy Wagner Wallis Director at the Baltimore Museum of Art

ALSO BY JOHN YAU

POETRY

Sometimes (1979)

Broken Off by the Music (1981)

Corpse and Mirror (1983)

Radiant Silhouette: New & Selected Work 1974-1988 (1989)

Big City Primer (1991), with photographs by Bill Barrette

Edificio Sayonara (1992)

Berlin Diptychon (1995), with photographs by Bill Barrette

Forbidden Entries (1996)

Borrowed Love Poems (2002)

Ing Grish (2005), with Thomas Nozkowski

Paradiso Diaspora (2006)

Further Adventures in Monochrome (2012)

Bijoux in the Dark (2018)

Genghis Chan on Drums (2021)

Tell It Slant (2023)

FICTION

The Sleepless Night of Eugene Delacroix (1980)

Hawaiian Cowboys (1995)

My Symptoms (1998)

My Heart Is That Eternal Rose Tattoo (2001)

CRITICISM

The Passionate Spectator: Essays on Art and Poetry (2006)

The Wild Children of William Blake (2017)

Foreign Sounds or Sounds Foreign (2020)

COLLABORATIONS

100 More Jokes from the Book of the Dead (2001), with Archie Rand

MONOGRAPHS

In the Realm of Appearances: The Art of Andy Warhol (1993)

A. R. Penck (1993)

Ed Moses: A Retrospective of Paintings and Drawings 1951–1996 (1996)

The United States of Jasper Johns (1996)

Pat Steir: Dazzling Water, Dazzling Light (2001)

Joan Mitchell: Works on Paper 1956–1992 (2007)

A Thing Among Things: The Art of Jasper Johns (2008)

William Tillyer: Watercolours (2010)

Jay DeFeo: Chiaroscuro (2013)

Richard Artschwager: Into the Desert (2015)

Catherine Murphy (2016)

Al Taylor: Early Paintings (2017)

Thomas Nozkowski (2017)

California Landscapes: Richard Diebenkorn / Wayne Thiebaud (2018)

Philip Taaffe (2018)

William Tillyer: A Retrospective (2021)

Liu Xiaodong (2021)

Joe Brainard: The Art of the Personal (2022)

AS EDITOR

Fairfield Porter: The Collected Poems with Selected Drawings (1985), with David Kermani

Fetish (1998)

PLEASE WAIT BY THE COATROOM

Please Wait by the Coatroom

Reconsidering Race and Identity in American Art

John Yau

Boston
BLACK SPARROW PRESS
2023

Published in 2023 by BLACK SPARROW PRESS

GODINE
Boston, Massachusetts
godine.com

LIBRARY OF CONGRESS CONTROL NUMBER 2022951486
ISBN 978-1-57423-261-5

First Printing, 2023
Printed in the United States of America

For Cerise Tzara Aschheim Yau

And all who were born into two worlds

CONTENTS

Introduction

WIFREDO ÓSCAR DE la Concepción Lam y Castilla, known as Wifredo Lam, was born in Sagua la Grande, Cuba, in 1902 and died in Paris, France, in 1982. His father, Yam Lam, was a Chinese immigrant, active in the island's Cantonese cultural community, and his mother, Ana Serafina Castilla, was the daughter of a Congolese formerly enslaved mother and a biracial Cuban father of African and European ancestry. I first learned of Lam and his racial identity when I was in high school, and was elated to discover an artist who was, like me, biracial Chinese. Although I had only seen a few paintings by Lam in black-and-white reproduction, I knew that his background must have influenced the choices he made in his art. I also knew that being biracial is complicated. What does it mean when you are not one, but two, and belong nowhere?

The erasure of Lam's biracial identity is why, more than twenty years after I discovered his work, I wrote, "Please Wait by the Coatroom: Wifredo Lam in the Museum of Modern Art" (*Arts Magazine*, December 1988). Were it not for Barry Schwabsky, a friend and the magazine's editor, who was enthusiastically receptive to my proposal, it is doubtful the article would have been published by any other New York art magazine. There was no exhibition of Lam to justify writing about him, and the art world's institutions were long satisfied with their judgement that he was a minor, derivative artist and second-rate Surrealist. In response to these assessments, I detailed in my article how grotesquely the museum and its curators had distorted Lam by treating him as if he were a white artist following in the steps of Pablo Picasso. A few hours after the issue came out, Barry called and told me that he had just learned that Lam's large gouache on paper *The Jungle* (1943)—the focus of my article—had been removed from the wall by the museum's entrance and put in storage. It was as if I had written about a painting that did not exist.

It was many years before the painting was seen again, near the men's room on the second floor of the new building designed by Yoshio Taniguchi. The museum's ongoing segregation of *The Jungle* prevented it from having a dialogue with Picasso's *Les Demoiselles d'Avignon* (1907), which I believe was Lam's original intention. The curators could not accept the possibility that Lam had reappropriated the African gods Picasso had appropriated at the beginning of the twentieth century, nor were they willing to entertain the idea that the purpose of his reappropriation was to restore, as well as give, the gods that Picasso had stolen a domain they could inhabit, undisturbed. Such thinking would mean recognizing that art was not a purely formal exploration, and that paint was not just paint. Placing Lam's *The Jungle* near Picasso's *Les Demoiselles d'Avignon* would challenge hierarchical thinking at the MoMA, where all the major artists are white.

I am not sure what I thought would happen when the article was published, but it was not avoidance from the MoMA. Nor did it stop there. The art world was silent, not only in response to my article but also to MoMA's swift removal of the painting. Not a single magazine or art writer commented on MoMA's decision. It was as if Lam and *The Jungle* had never existed, and to a large degree he did not, except perhaps as a footnote to Pablo Picasso.

Three years later, it was wonderfully affirming when my essay was included in the anthology *Out There: Marginalization and Contemporary Culture* (1992). And yet it seemed to me that the mainstream art world was still not interested in the issues I had raised.

I felt like I was talking to myself in a noisy tunnel full of people rushing about because they had more important things on their mind. MoMA's response and the art world's subsequent silence helped deepen my resolve to address the aesthetics of exclusion, and the manifold ways it has been maintained, like a well-oiled machine. I also knew that I had to be stealthy about it.

In order to confront and expose what I felt were widespread omissions and gross misrepresentations, as well as protect myself, I always tried to remember what the Black curator Lowery Stokes Sims said to me after I got particularly heated in a public discussion: "You have to pick your battles." I had just disagreed with a prominent white art critic, who dismissed what I had to say about racial identity with arrogant disdain: "I don't think about what color I am when I get up in the morning. I wash my face and brush my teeth." The contempt in his response was blatant, but the gist of it was not surprising, as I had experienced being brushed aside before and knew that it would happen again.

This book chronicles some of the battles that I have chosen to fight, starting with "Please Wait by the Coatroom" and continuing on to articles published more recently.

As a poet interested in Surrealism and Dada, I was always on the lookout for books on the subject. That is why I picked up the MoMA publication *Dada, Surrealism, and their Heritage* (1968) when—in the mid-1980s—I saw it for sale in a bargain book bin at the Strand Bookstore, whose slogan is "18 miles of books." This is where I (and other New York creatives) went to look for remaindered and discounted books, and where I found rare and out-of-print monographs and catalogs for a low price. While reading a description of Lam and his work in *Dada, Surrealism, and their Heritage*, I discovered indisputable proof of what I knew had always been there: the art world's blanket denial of the role that ethnicity can play in the formation of one's aesthetic choices. In that not-so-long-ago time, quality was all that mattered and artists were colorless—meaning white. While some perceptions have been modified, I believe that artists of color have still not gained parity with white artists, who are considered the groundbreakers.

In order to frame my objection to this hierarchical thinking, I chose to write about MoMA's placement of *The Jungle* on the wall leading to the museum's coatroom, hence the title.

Even though he was antagonistic toward Surrealism because he did not think it was as formally innovative as Cubism, William S. Rubin organized the exhibition *Dada, Surrealism, and their Heritage* (1968) for MoMA, paving the way for him to join the museum's staff as a permanent curator and promote his formalist agenda. This is the offending entry he wrote about Lam in the exhibition catalogue:

> Wifredo Lam was the first Surrealist to make primitive and ethnic sources central to his art.

Rubin erased Lam's ethnicity as well as his familiarity with Yoruba religious practices, which started when he was a child, as well as downplayed Surrealism's contribution to art.

As I dug deeper into the few pieces of critical writing on Lam by American scholars, I discovered that those writings were very different from what was written about him in France. I learned it wasn't just Rubin who'd rejected Lam's complex heritage. Nor was Lam's case an isolated example. Rather, I found that Rubin's cleaving of identity and aesthetics was a common practice in the American art world. By the standards of objectivity that were being widely used to determine an artwork's quality, Lam was judged to be a derivative white or colorless artist patterning himself after Pablo Picasso. Rubin considered Lam's identity, which was an amalgamation of Asian, European, and African lineages, irrelevant to his art, and he was hardly alone. These so-called objective viewpoints were espoused by Clement Greenberg, Donald Judd, Rosalind Krauss, and others in high positions of authority. That mindset helped establish, develop, and preserve the rules used to conclude what was groundbreaking and important about avant-garde art, especially in New York—and one's racial identity was considered irrelevant to one's art.

The subversion of this thinking became my unannounced, self-appointed task: I had to find ways to expose the mechanisms that enabled the mainstream art world to go blithely along, content that it was examining everything with the same detached, objective eye, while ignoring formative issues such as identity and cultural background. As I wrote about artists as racially and culturally diverse as Ruth Asawa, Richard Hunt, James Luna, Jiha Moon, Nadia Haji Omar, and Kerry James Marshall, I repeatedly realized how complicated and nuanced identity can be, particularly in the ways artists manifest it in their work. There is no one-size-fits-all approach to studying the work of these artists, as exemplified by the various strains of formalist criticism that for a long time dominated the art world's assessments. Just as each artist's work calls for a germane response, writing about a body of work meant you had to see what they were doing with your own eyes, unguided by the marketplace or the opinions of others.

By writing about the work of artists of different ethnicities and cultures, I came to realize that race was not monolithic and that identity was not a fixed and reductive form, however much the art world might wish it were so. Rather, identity was something that was constantly changing, at least in the artists that I chose to write about, because a significant number of them were biracial. They experienced the world through the overlapping yet distinct lenses of their multiple legacies and histories. The art world—like the larger world it is part of—is not made up of only Black and white artists.

When Kerry James Marshall stated, "One of the reasons I paint Black people is because I am a Black person . . . There are fewer representations of Black figures in the historical record," he made a point that I want to expand upon. Isn't Marshall's statement also applicable to artists of other colors, races, and ethnicities living in America? Doesn't it also apply to biracial artists? Haven't these artists also been waiting by the coatroom, denied full entry by museums and other art-world institutions? It is this world of closed doors—which I and many others have lived in and worked with our entire lives—that I have tried to address in the essays that I selected for this book.

I moved to New York in the mid-1970s and began to write about art shortly afterward. For years, I was only allowed to write about artists that no one else wanted to write about. This was the first glass ceiling that I was aware of encountering in the art world. Despite this and other obstacles, I realized that in order to push back against the art world's blindness about race, ethnicity, and non-white cultures, I had to begin disassembling the structures of thinking and seeing that were in place. I knew that I had to begin "collecting my own stories" before they were further ignored or erased, as Amy Fung writes in her book *Before I Was a Critic I Was a Human Being*, which I review in this collection. What I take Fung to mean by "stories" is that you have to learn how to listen to others, and to hear what they have to say. It also means that you have to start fresh and learn to see through your own eyes. This book is a record of my repeated attempts to do what all people, including art critics, should do: look for themselves and see what is actually there.

PLEASE WAIT BY THE COATROOM

I.

Please Wait by the Coatroom

Wifredo Lam in the Museum of Modern Art

THE MUSEUM OF Modern Art's carefully orchestrated presentation of its permanent collection of painting and sculpture is based on the paradigm of the textbook. Located on the museum's second floor, the ordered succession of the gallery spaces underscores the belief that the history of modern art can be reduced to a verifiable narrative. Under the authorship of William S. Rubin, who was the director of the department of painting and sculpture at MoMA from 1973 to 1988, the museum organized and mounted exhibitions that further defined and clarified a reading of history: *Dada, Surrealism, and Their Heritage* (1968); *Frank Stella* (1969); *Andre Masson* (1976); *Pablo Picasso* (1980); *"Primitivism" in 20th Century Art* (1984); *Richard Serra* (1984); *Frank Stella* (1987). Each of the exhibitions was accompanied by a text that marshaled together essays, reproductions, and documents in support of the curator's purposeful reading of history. Besides being a textbook—one that is backed by the "facts"—the museum is also a factory that produces textbooks, simultaneously documenting and legitimizing its presentations.

During his tenure, Rubin defined his department's project as the evaluation and systematizing of art history. The result: a rigid codification of the past; a formalist reading of how the past intersects the present; a hierarchical encoding of the present. The historical continuity the museum, specifically Rubin's department, has both delineated and perpetuated is most clearly evident in the two large retrospectives it has devoted to documenting Frank Stella's career. Rubin has used his position to make the museum Stella's strongest advocate. Instead of creating a place where the artist can present his or her propositions, both the museum's facilities (gallery space and publication department) and Rubin (curator and author) have elected themselves to argue the artist's importance.

The museum's propositions have repeatedly attempted to establish, stabilize, oversee, and ensure a strict, hierarchical encoding of art history based on formalist notions of originality and connoisseurship. Given the Museum of Modern Art's status within contemporary cultural discourse, perhaps it is time to begin examining Rubin's reading of history. The purpose of the examination is simply to expose the narrative of exclusion that Rubin—with the approval of many others—has assembled over the past two decades.

Wifredo Lam's *The Jungle* (1943) hangs in the hallway leading to the museum's coatroom. Its location is telling. The artist's work has been allowed into the museum's lobby, but, like a delivery boy, has been made to stand and hold the package in an inconspicuous passageway near the door. By denying Lam and his work the possibility of going upstairs and conversing with Cezanné, Picasso, Matisse, Jackson Pollock, Morris Louis, and Kenneth Noland (their works are carefully arranged on the walls of the main galleries), the museum relegates both the artist and his work to secondary status.

The Jungle is slightly larger than life-size. Done in gouache, which is a fast-drying, water-based medium, Lam's carefully entangled, translucent composition converts the act of viewing into the process of sorting out and identifying the painting's constituents. The dominant color is a glowing, midnight blue—we have left the world of daylight and entered the domain of dreams. The composition is horizontally divided into two roughly equal areas. In the upper half, where four faces are delineated, the figures (their limbs) unfold across the surface as well as emerge from and sink back into the densely layered foliage (ovoid leaves and segmented bamboo canes) of a "jungle" that exists in the artist's imagination, as there is no counterpart to this painted landscape in Cuba. The spatially more open lower half consists of a face in the lower left-hand corner, elongated limbs, and monumental feet, which are pointing back or away from the viewer.

Counterpointing the dense array of verticals and ovoids in the painting's upper half, the lower half's recessive spatiality is a formal device that seems to permit the viewer entry into the composition. The limbs and huge feet, however, become stumbling blocks. At the same time, the combination of their placement and the frontality of the faces evokes a specific moment; they have stopped whatever it was they were doing to gaze out at us. The composition is meant to be confrontational.

Lam's emphasis of blue does not allow a realistic reading of the scene. His use of lighter or different tones to accent the faces and limbs corresponds to the composition's interior logic. By repeating and overlapping the feet, Lam conveys the possibility that the painting is not a scene; it is a hallucination. We are not seeing the painting; we are dreaming it. Thrust forward, on the upper right side, is a hand holding a pair of large shears. We may wish to cut through this dream, but we cannot. Instead, the faces look through us, as if we were nothing more than insubstantial presences. One could say the tables have been turned. They (the figures that are embedded in the composition) have more power than the viewer. Unable to enter the spatial domain of which they are the rulers, we viewers remain in our own world. Meanwhile, they remain unmoved by our presence.

Wifredo Lam (1902–82) was born in Cuba, the son of a Chinese father and an Afro-Cuban mother. According to Lam, his mother told him that one of his ancestors was a cimarrøn, a runaway slave, named José Castilla. After Castilla killed a man and went into hiding, he was nicknamed "Mano Cortado" (Chopped Hand). The other influence on Lam was his godmother, Mantønica Wilson, a

Yoruba priestess. Because of her reputation as a sorcerer and healer, Lam was able to participate in various religious ceremonies. It was Wilson who introduced him to such figures as Shango, the mythical ancestor of the Yorubas—the master of thunder.

In 1918, Lam sailed to Spain, where he attended art school and, later, began gaining a reputation as an artist. He fought and was wounded in the Spanish Civil War. In 1938, after recovering from his wound, he went to Paris, where he met Picasso. In 1940, after France's defeat and the German occupation of Paris, he reacquainted himself with such friends as André Breton, Victor Brauner, and Óscar Domínguez. In 1941, he embarked for Martinique with Breton, Claude Lévi-Strauss, and more than three hundred others on the *Capitaine Pail-Merle*.

Lam's odyssey lasted more than seven months, including a detention on Martinique for more than a month. While he was incarcerated, he met and formed a lasting relationship with the poet Aimé Césaire, one of the founders of the Négritude movement. Before leaving Martinique, Lam provided the illustrations for Césaire's *Cahier D'un Retour Au Pays Natal* (*Notebook of a Return to the Native Land*). It is in this journal that the word Négritude appeared for the first time in a poem:

> My negritude is not a stone, its deafness hurled against
> the clamor of the day
> my negritude is not a leukoma of dead liquid over the
> earth's dead eye
> my negritude is neither tower nor cathedral[1]

For both Lam and Césaire, their return to a native land was a symbolic journey and an actual one.

In an interview with Max-Pol Fouchet, Lam described the Cuba he returned to in the early 1940s:

> Poetry in Cuba then was either political and committed, like that of Nicolás Guillén and a few others, or else written for tourists. The latter I rejected, for it had nothing do with an exploited people, with a society that

> crushed and humiliated its slaves. No, I decided that my painting would never be the equivalent of that pseudo-Cuban music for nightclubs. I refused to paint cha-cha-cha. I wanted with all my heart to paint the drama of my country, but by thoroughly expressing the Black spirit, the beauty of the plastic arts of the Blacks. In this way I could act as a Trojan horse that would spew forth hallucinating figures with the power to surprise, to disturb the dreams of the explorers. I knew that I was running the risk of not being understood by either the man in the street or by others. But the true picture has to set the imagination to work, even if it takes time.

As Lam saw it, his aesthetic/social project was to faithfully express the spirit of being Black, which rejected colonialist thinking. Among other things, this meant that he had to find a way to be faithful to the original meaning and power of the plastic arts of his Afro-Cuban culture. Painted shortly after he returned to Cuba, *The Jungle* is Lam's creative-critical manifesto; it embodies his response to both accepted art practices and to being a descendant of a slave culture, something that Rubin chooses to ignore.[2]

The Museum of Modern Art's placement of *The Jungle* is influenced by Rubin's evaluation of Lam's achievement. In tacit support of his judgment, the museum has published two very similar readings of Lam's work, the first in 1968 and the second in 1984, meaning that nothing had changed in their thinking. In *Dada, Surrealism, and Their Heritage* (1968; 2nd edition, 1977), Rubin wrote an entry of six sentences on Lam:

> Wifredo Lam was the first Surrealist to make primitive and ethnic sources central to his art. Though we see iconographical traces of such magical imagery from time to time in the work of Ernst, it counted for surprisingly little among the Surrealist painters in general. This despite the fact that many Surrealists were avid collectors of primitive art, which appealed to them because it stood *outside of an aesthetic tradition*. [. . .] Picasso was one of the earliest and continuous influences on Lam, and many of his forests reflect the shallow space and hybrid iconography of *Les Demoiselles*.[3]

In Volume II of *"Primitivism" in 20th Century Art: Affinity of the Tribal and Modern* (1984, edited by William S. Rubin), Evan Maurer, in his essay, "Dada and Surrealism," makes the following observations: "This was Lam's greatest synthesis as a Surrealist: He combined a close contact with tribal rituals with the cultural and artistic sophistication of a Western intellectual," which is another way of saying that Lam thought like an educated white man.[4]

Maurer goes on to state:

> *The Jungle* summarizes not only Lam's use of Primitive imagery but his debt to Picasso, whom he looked upon as both teacher and kindred spirit. Its dense foliage is peopled by four totemlike figures who stand in the foreground of the typically shallow, nonillusionistic space, Lam's homage to both the common "reductiveness" of Primitive art and Picasso's *Les Demoiselles d'Avignon.*

As Rubin and Maurer see it, Lam was unable to emerge from the influence of Picasso, and *The Jungle* is his homage to *Les Demoiselles d'Avignon,* the first painting of the twentieth century to incorporate imagery derived from African sculpture. Moreover, neither of them seems to think that Lam's heritage, something he himself cites, is important. In their eyes, he is simply a "white" Cuban who went to Europe and became an uninventive Surrealist, a synthesizer. They cannot conceive of him wanting to develop an alternative vision of history.[5]

Does *The Jungle* pay homage as well as owe a debt to *Les Demoiselles d'Avignon,* as Maurer states and Rubin implies? Or is it a purposeful reevaluation and critique of Picasso's painting? From their comparable sizes and similar placement of figures, it is clear that *Les Demoiselles d'Avignon* was very much on Lam's mind when he began *The Jungle*. In fact, Lam's painting is directed toward Picasso's. The message it embodies, however, is neither self-diminishing nor an homage. Instead, it represents a conscious opposition to Picasso's influence and practice.

Picasso's five women are standing or seated within the reception area of a brothel. The woman on the far left, the only one not staring down at the viewer, has just drawn back the curtain. Shamelessly naked, the other four are either "posing" or "exhibiting" themselves. Rising up from the middle of the bottom edge is a table, a still life of fruits balanced on it. The painting imaginatively records a specific moment in a narrative. After entertaining the customer (the viewer), the woman on the far right has gotten up and pulled back the curtain. Which of the four women do we want? It is a confrontation between desire (the act of looking) and implacability.

Started as an allegory about venereal disease, Picasso's painting has escaped its moralizing message and become something else. A standoff between the women (the objects of desire and therefore representations of the painting itself) and the viewer (the customer who wishes to possess one of the objects, part of the painting, but cannot), it is an all-or-nothing struggle that the prostitutes always win. They remain in their world, while we return to ours after having viewed them (the women) and it (the painting).

Lam's painting posits an entirely different order. The setting is derived from nature, but its composition is not a naturalistic description: it is a made-up world. The confrontation is psychic. Neither friendly nor antagonistic, but rather simply alien or other, his female figures exist in another world. Whereas Picasso overcomes Christianity, Lam does not feel compelled to consider it. His rendering of the Senufo figures is not due to a lack of inventiveness: it is an act of faith and faithfulness to these gods.

Within the terms proposed by Lam's artistic practice, the African figures are not "reductive" artifacts to be absorbed into Western perceptual systems, such as Cubism. Instead, they are presences existing in the here and now. Picasso is able to use them only when he attaches their faces to the women's bodies. Lam, on the other hand, does not appropriate them. He restores them. *The Jungle* represents a turning point in Lam's career. From 1943 on, he constantly re-presents himself in direct opposition to Picasso and the colonialist appropriation of his birthright. By the 1960s, he had dispensed with the jungle setting altogether. Emerging from and sinking back into the moody atmospheric grounds, the figures' attenuated presences are never subjected to an overall design. Their unfolding, overlapping limbs and torsos argue against a detached viewing of them. They exist somewhere between a multi-limbed ideogram and a haunting presence.

The Museum of Modern Art's judgment of Lam is based on a centrist, linear reading of art history. In their approach to art, Rubin and Maurer value formal innovation over style, and style over iconography. Consequently, they believe that subject matter, which might be defined as the translation of the hybrid ingredients of consciousness into visual evidence, is of little importance, since the aesthetic tradition of Western art can only be renewed when an individual makes a formal breakthrough. They both define and use the sign of "originality" to determine their judgments. They are not interested in an individual trying to rebuild a world that was taken from him both literally and aesthetically.

By designating Lam as "the first Surrealist to make primitive and ethnic sources central to his art," Rubin deprives the artist of his birthright. Instead of addressing the issues raised by Lam's response to a slave culture and colonialism, Rubin writes about him as if he were a generic Caucasian artist working in the tradition of appropriated primitive iconography. Had Rubin been sensitive to cultural differences, oppositional stances, and the attempt to come to terms with one's cross-cultural identity, he might have written: *Born in Cuba, which is part of the Americas, Wifredo Lam is the first modernist artist to emphasize his African descent by transforming his personal awareness of such cultural practices as colonialism and ongoing Yoruba religious rituals into a contemporary mode of expression.* Such a sentence would have suggested that an artist of African descent could enter into the cultural discourse as an equal. Additionally, it would have revealed an awareness of the dominant culture's need to examine its own practices. Finally, it would have enlarged the continually shifting geopolitical, social, and aesthetic boundaries of Western art, as well as introduced Lam into the canon as a unique individual.

The writings of Rubin and Maurer are acts of transgression. They see in Lam only what is in their own eyes: colorless or white artists. They feel secure in approaching him with an a priori discourse that focuses on similarities rather than explores differences. For Lam to achieve the status of a unique individual, he would have had to successfully adapt to the conditions of imprisonment (the aesthetic standards of a fixed tradition) that they and others construct and watch over. To enter this prison, which takes the alluring form of museums, art history textbooks, galleries, and magazines, an individual must suppress cultural differences and become a colorless ghost. The bind every hybrid American artist must deal with is this: Should they investigate the constantly changing polymorphous conditions affecting identity, tradition, and reality? Or should they choose to assimilate into the mainstream art world by focusing on approved aesthetic issues? Instead of assimilating, Lam infiltrated the aesthetic rules governing the pictorial conventions of "the exploiters." He became, as he says, "a Trojan horse."

The two entries on Wifredo Lam represent a miniscule portion of everything the Museum of Modern Art has published. And yet, might not these misguided evaluations of him suggest the fallibility inherent in much of the accepted approaches to art? And might not this errant thinking raise certain questions that the institutions and individuals of the art world have consistently failed to address? In fact, might not the entire process by which we determine which artists have made significant contributions to culture be questionable?

Césaire showed Lam another side of the relationship between a slave culture and a colonial one. After Lam returned to Cuba and witnessed the ongoing effects of "a society that crushed and humiliated its slaves," he saw Picasso through different eyes. The sanitizing responses of Rubin and Maurer reverse Lam's intentions. This reversal is doubled by the museum's placement and mislabeling. The label never mentions that Lam worked in Cuba.

After Lam perceived Picasso to be an artist-colonialist, he defined himself as an artist-restorer and began demanding parity. He did so by re-appropriating the African gods that Picasso first appropriated in 1907, and restoring them to their rightful domain. Painting was the only world they could still rule. *The Jungle* belongs on the wall opposite *Les Demoiselles d'Avignon.* The argument Lam started with Picasso goes beyond either of them. But in 1988, almost fifty years after Lam began to paint on behalf of his culture, the Museum of Modern Art has failed to acknowledge its existence.

II.

Rethinking Isamu Noguchi's Greatness

IT IS APPARENT from his 1926 Guggenheim Fellowship application that Isamu Noguchi had developed a revolutionary conception of sculpture early in his career. He went to Paris in 1927 and worked for a short time in the studio of Constantin Brancusi, whose work he had seen in an exhibition in New York. While it is clear that the exhibition had a profound effect on Noguchi, I think it is too confining to see Brancusi's influence as solely stylistic, or only in terms of Noguchi's move toward abstraction. Rather, Brancusi's exhibition offered a fresh and inspiring perspective on Noguchi's biracial heritage and his childhood in Japan, where he learned about traditional wood joinery. This is how he declared his radical view in his application, which the Guggenheim Foundation approved:

> It is my desire to view nature through nature's eyes, and to ignore man as a special object of veneration. There must be unthought of heights of beauty to which sculpture may be raised by this reversal of attitude.

He also stated:

> My father, Yone Noguchi, is Japanese and has long been known as an interpreter of the East to the West, through poetry. I wish to do the same through sculpture.

By placing "nature" and "nature's eyes" at the center of his approach, Noguchi consciously rejected Realism, Symbolism, Cubism, and the concept of artist as omnipotent author. While still in his early twenties, he seemed to have recognized the necessity of resisting the traditions we associate with Auguste Rodin, Aristide Maillol, Jacques Lipchitz, and Pablo Picasso (in his work with Julio González). The likely reason that Noguchi rejected these approaches was because they would have required him to assimilate into a Western tradition, which he, as someone who was biracial, must have recognized was impossible. More importantly, he would have had to suppress the complexities of his mixed heritage.

Noguchi's "reversal" was likely influenced by his childhood in Japan. At the age of nine, he worked closely with a carpenter to build a wooden house for himself and his mother using traditional materials and methods of construction, such as joinery. The house was built without nails, bricks, or concrete. This and other early formative experiences helped shape his aesthetic viewpoint, which was a unique synthesis of East and West. And yet, paradoxical as it may sound, Noguchi's genius went beyond a blend of East and West to fuse a wide range of seemingly incompatible experiences and discrete influences into a flexible approach.

At the same time, as a counterpoint to his imaginative synthesis, we should recognize that another motivating factor was his deep estrangement and underlying sense of discomfort, as culturally speaking he did not belong anywhere. As he said in an interview with Paul Cummings: "I get [. . .] discontented with my situation and want to break out." Noguchi's discontent and subsequent restlessness helps explain the diversity of his oeuvre, which includes domestic objects and recreation areas: it is a testament to his willingness to take on new challenges.[1]

Certainly, Noguchi's astonishing ability to work across disciplines has contributed to our inability to grasp the fullness of his achievement, which extends from the field of design (lamps, chairs, tables, and chess sets) to public parks, gardens, children's playgrounds, and swimming pools, and from carving directly in stone to envisioning a *Sculpture to Be Seen from Mars* (1947). I cannot think of another twentieth-century sculptor who took on as many projects, materials, and processes as Noguchi did during the course of his career, which spanned seven decades.

Noguchi was born in 1904 in Los Angeles, California, to a Japanese poet, Yonejiro (Yone) Noguchi, and an American editor and writer, Léonie Gilmour. Rejected by his father, who returned to Japan and soon after married a Japanese wife, Noguchi moved to Japan with his mother when he was an infant. He lived there until he was thirteen, at which point, obeying his mother's wishes, he returned to America on his own and went to school in Indiana. Sailing to America by himself, Noguchi understandably felt rejected by both of his parents. These feelings of rejection were further enhanced by a world where anti-miscegenation laws were in force in many places, and interracial marriages were looked down upon. Nearly everywhere he went, Noguchi was prone to feeling like an outcast, especially in America and Japan. Although he felt discarded by his parents and unwanted by the world, he was able to make his way. In hindsight, it should be apparent how miraculous Noguchi's life journey and career were.

According to Bruce Altshuler, in his indispensable monograph:

> Noguchi said that he could feel at home everywhere because he was at home nowhere, and this issue became a central theme of his life and work. His sense of homelessness and his longing to redress it became a source both for his creation of places for social connection and interaction and for some of his most poignant carving.[2]

Noguchi's sense "that he could feel at home everywhere because he was at home nowhere" echoes Charles Baudelaire's description of the perfect flâneur:

> To be away from home and yet to feel oneself everywhere at home; to see the world, to be at the center of the

> world, and yet to remain hidden from the world—such are a few of the slightest pleasures of those independent, passionate, impartial natures which the tongue can but clumsily define.

The difference is that Noguchi's feelings of estrangement began with his mixed heritage. The crowd was not his element, which helps us understand why he was interested in making work, especially civic-minded environments, where private contemplation and "social connection and interaction" were not mutually exclusive. He was cognizant of the possibility that the individual may not feel like being part of a crowd, and that introspection and privacy could be sustaining. For Noguchi, "social connection and interaction" had their basis in conversation and face-to-face encounters, as his many designs for tables attest.[3]

Influenced by his close relationships with such prominent figures as Brancusi (in whose Paris studio he worked for three months), the utopian architect and thinker R. Buckminster Fuller, the choreographer and dancer Martha Graham (for whom he designed stage sets and costumes), the stone carver Masatoshi Izumi (with whom he began collaborating with in the 1960s), and the architect Gordon Bunshaft (with whom he worked on a number of public projects), Noguchi developed ideas about modern art that dissolved the boundaries between art and design, between sculpture and environment, and between ancient stone carving and modern processes and materials. Rather than feeling blocked by his profound sense of alienation, Noguchi became an expansive, innovative artist who ignored boundaries, continually redrawing the map that conventionally separated design from sculpture, objects from the surrounding space, and public projects from playgrounds for children. One senses that Noguchi was committed to the possibility that anything and anyplace could be transformed into an aesthetic object or environment, and that he reached this understanding without being influenced by the Bauhaus.

This aptly titled exhibition, *Variations*, focuses on sculptures, models for public projects, and designs. The exhibition includes works on paper made in the late 1920s, while Noguchi was living in Paris, as well as models for playgrounds and sculptural objects for the stage, which he made in the 1940s, and sculptures that he carved in stone in the late 1980s, during the last years of his life. The emphasis of the exhibition is on the abstract work that Noguchi made while in Paris and took up again in the early 1940s, after working as a portrait sculptor of busts during the 1930s.

Equally comfortable in stone, wood, steel, bronze, glass, and plastic, Noguchi mastered the use of premodern tools (hammer, axe, and chisel) as well as modern ones (welder and acetylene torch). Noguchi's mastery of these seemingly incommensurable methods and materials sets his work apart from the welded steel sculptures of his contemporary, David Smith; it also challenges the notion that an artist must work only with the tools of his or her time. If anything, Noguchi was a modern master who made use of the most ancient of all materials: stone.

If Noguchi's profound feelings of separation inspired him to address situations both domestic and public, the breadth of his achievement can be viewed in terms of discovering imaginative ways to remake the world that we routinely inhabit, from the personal to the civic. It is this breadth that makes Noguchi a unique figure, one who saw everything that touched on where and how we live as subject matter. In this regard, Noguchi's achievement is unrivaled and not yet widely recognized in America, particularly in the commercial art world, which has cared more for the work of David Smith and Richard Serra.

In his gouaches on paper, collectively titled *Paris Abstractions*, all of which date from 1928, the year after he arrived in Paris and briefly worked in Brancusi's studio, it is readily apparent that he has absorbed the older artist's reductive vision, as well as moved away from it. Noguchi's abstract drawings, in flat black-and-white gouache, play off organic and geometric forms, and also line and shape.

In the tension between two different vocabularies, the organic and the geometric, Altshuler sees:

> This dynamic between two kinds of imagery [as] the first instance of what would become an essential aspect of Noguchi's mature work: his tolerance for, and use of, polarity. Though related to his bicultural background, his use of dichotomy extended far beyond the combining of East and West to include his choice of themes and working processes. In his use of opposites—sometimes blending, sometimes alternating them—Noguchi was able to make use of more materials and more different ways of working than those taking a less diverse course.

A list of some of the materials that Noguchi used in the work included in *Variations* confirms Altshuler's point: hot-dipped galvanized steel; stainless steel; bronze; iron; basalt; different kinds of granite; different kinds of wood; cast aluminum; plexiglass and other kinds of plastic; fabric tape; mosaic tiles; plywood; paint; plaster; marble; clay; glass.[4]

Noguchi's range calls to mind a distinction that Baudelaire made in "The Painter of Modern Life" between the "cosmopolitan" and the "artist." In contrast to the "cosmopolitan," or man of the world, the "artist," or narrow specialist, "is wedded to his palette like the serf to the soil." In addition to this distinction, Baudelaire identifies a crisis that is central to modernism: one need not be confined to one material or process. By not restricting himself to a particular medium, material, or process, Noguchi anticipated the postmodern artist. Moreover, in both his plans for public parks and those he was able to complete, he anticipated earthworks and other large-scale art projects that involve altering or intervening in the landscape.[5]

One of the distinguishing features of Noguchi's work is his investigation of the relationship between objects and gravity. He does not confine this exploration to sculpture. In his design for *Coffee Table* (1944–73), he placed a glass tabletop on top of two identical biomorphic shapes, one of which is inverted and partially balanced by the other. The two shapes remind us of our essential connection to nature, that we cannot isolate ourselves from it, even when we are sitting in our apartment. By designing a table in which interdependence plays a central role, Noguchi calls attention to the contingent: everything is conditional and therefore subject to change, even something as static as a glass and walnut coffee table. At the same time, the glass top allows us to see what is lifting it into the air, helping it to hover. Whereas in the West art and life are seen as separate domains, Noguchi wanted to return us to that moment when they were inseparable, as they were when he lived in a house made without nails, where everything was fitted together.

Not one to repeat an idea until it becomes entrenched as a style, Noguchi designed another table out of gray granite formed into a circle: *Garden Table* (1983) floats just above a green lawn, evoking what is beneath it, even as it seems to deny its weighty materiality. In his explorations of the relationship between weight and weightlessness, solidity and fragility, Noguchi has made work out of stone that seems to simultaneously acknowledge and defy gravity.

In the marble sculpture *Awakening* (1987), Noguchi carves a notched column that seems to be twisting ever so slightly, endowing it with a sense of movement and change. His ability to undermine stone, to imbue it with qualities we would never otherwise associate with it, is a hallmark of his genius. It is hardly the only one.

The iron sculpture *Endless Coupling* (1957), made the year that Brancusi died, pays homage to the erotic side of Noguchi's mentor, which was expressed in such works as *The Kiss* (1907–08) and the scandalous, phallic shaped, *Princess X* (1920). As the title makes apparent, *Endless Coupling* is the inseparable joining of two different columnar forms, a frank celebration of sexual union. It is like an adagio act that never succumbs to gravity.

In *The Opening* (1970), which is made of French rose marble and Italian white marble, Noguchi makes a column of white and rose sections that bends over, like a gymnast, until it forms an arch. One of the remarkable things about *The Opening* is that each rose and white section is distinct, that nothing is repeated. Although the piece is entirely abstract, only someone who has paid attention to dancers and other athletic figures could have made that shape. One senses a tension between the archlike shape and the impulse toward verticality; it is as if the piece fell over, which is impossible. *The Opening* never becomes static, never settles into a comfortable position. The irresolvable tension between discomfort and gracefulness the viewer encounters in *The Opening* is particular to Noguchi's work and no one else's.

Brancusi, who never became a Cubist, was one of the first sculptors to make abstract sculpture. Working largely in stone and wood, he relied on traditional tools such as a hammer and chisel. His approach was meticulous and inclusive. In his attention to the base or pedestal on which his sculptures rested, and in his use of a modular, infinitely repeatable unit, he is widely regarded as paving the way for Minimalism. This is how Carl Andre described Brancusi's importance: "I think I could have done my work if Duchamp had not lived. I could not have done my work if Brancusi had not lived."[6]

While Brancusi's importance to Minimalism cannot be overstated, it seems to me that the commonplace narrative linking them together ignores a more complex possibility. For one thing, this narrative emphasizes an inexorable move away from craftsmanship and traditional materials, such as stone and wood, to fabrication and modern materials, such as steel and lead. Within this telling, the history of the discrete abstract sculpture begins with Brancusi, passes through David Smith, and culminates with the Minimalists before being redefined by Rosalind Krauss as "sculpture in the expanded field." It seems to me that there is another narrative, which has been ignored. Noguchi—in his use of premodern tools and his devotion to traditional craftsmanship, such as stone carving—can be said to advance Brancusi's legacy without aligning himself with the reductive impulse associated with Minimalism, as well as anticipate the work of Martin Puryear, whose devotion to traditional craft is a hallmark of his art.

Rather than bringing about the cessation of art devoted to craftsmanship, as Minimalism was thought to have done, artists who relied on their hands presented a challenge to that narrative. Noguchi, now in his later years and working in stone, bronze, and stainless steel, clearly proved that he was up to the task, creating such varied sculptures as the floor piece *Resonance* (1985) and the vertical *Open Column* (1958–73). Isn't it time to rethink our assumptions about modern and postmodern art, as well as the paradigms of progress and culmination used to assess innovation? Shouldn't we look again at the work of one of the greatest sculptors of the twentieth century?

Ruth Asawa's Life Masks

RUTH ASAWA'S AUTONOMY is inseparable from her art. As she was never one to connect her self-worth to the art world's judgments, or to accede to its commercial demands, her work extends beyond the hanging wire sculptures that first gained her attention in the burgeoning New York art world of the 1950s.

In 1960, Asawa and her husband, Albert Lanier, purchased a cedar-shingled house in Noe Valley, where they lived the rest of their lives. Moving into a new house, which Lanier enlarged so that it could accommodate their family, Asawa had a large studio workshop for the first time. Marilyn Chase wrote about the home in her biography *Everything She Touched: The Life of Ruth Asawa* (2020):

> The studio workshop accommodated Ruth's artistic output. And the house inspired and invited her to pursue two additional art forms: hand-carved wooden doors and life masks, which adorned the exterior. For the entrance, Ruth began carving massive redwood double doors with an abstract design of interlocking waves and whorls, a pattern reminiscent of [Josef] Albers's design class exercises known as "meanders."

Living in her own house—where she could make art, cultivate a garden, and have enough room for the family to be comfortable—

Asawa seems to have wanted to do two things in carving the doors and, a few years after moving in, making life masks of family and friends and others who came to visit. By carving the doors, Asawa welcomed visitors into a sanctuary that she and her family established. It was also about exerting control over the structure that she and her family lived in, which would have been important to Asawa, whose family had been barred from owning property and then uprooted by the United States government and confined to internment camps during World War II.

Cast from the faces of family members, friends, guests, and students, the life masks are a sculptural diary of the people in Asawa and her family's life, as well as a chronicle of a community's existence in time. Mounted on the outside of the shingled house, they became welcome signs, a record of the people Asawa had known and interacted with, as well as protective spirits. Asawa eventually placed more than 250 life masks on the exterior wall.

If the wire sculptures were meant to go out into the world, the doors and life masks were not. According to Chase, "Life-casting sessions became a regular feature of the Laniers' social gatherings. Guests would lie down while Ruth framed their faces with cardboard and coated their skin with Vaseline. . . . When dry, the [plaster] cast became a mold for the mask."

In order to grasp what is truly radical and innovative about Asawa and her work, I think it is important that we consider her diverse oeuvre in its entirety, which includes—in addition to the looped wire sculptures—life masks, doors, and different bodies of drawings. Looking at these discrete groups of work, we realize that Asawa used direct processes that recognized the innate properties of her materials; she carved wood, bent and twisted wire, casted a face, molded clay, and drew every day, often in ink during the early morning before her family was awake and after the family had dinner.

In the mid-1960s, when the art world's attention was shifting toward fabrication and the use of ready-mades, Asawa learned how to make life masks from George Neal, a high school art teacher in San Francisco. By this time, she was well into what Chase called "her second vocation: promoting art in public schools." Asawa's interest in learning a hands-on technique from Neal underscores what we should keep in mind about Asawa: always her own person, she was motivated by something larger than achieving success in the New York art world. And that something was a belief that art is an engagement that helps people become aware of the material world they inhabit and unlock their creative potential. She embodied a sense of creativity and community that goes beyond the one defined by Donald Judd, who emphasized the new in this way in his influential essay "Specific Objects" (1965): "Most of the work involves new materials, either recent inventions or things not used before in art." More than parting company with Judd, Asawa reminds us that the purpose of art need not be limited to embracing what is upheld as avant-garde or to supporting capitalism's emphasis on the new.

In his essay for Asawa's 1973 retrospective for the San Francisco Museum of Art, Gerald Nordland wrote:

> As the result of studying a 1963 issue of *Life* magazine devoted to Roman busts, masks and likenesses, Asawa interested herself in making life masks of her friends. At one time she had the idea of making 10,000 masks but to date she has fallen short of that goal. She became fascinated by the uniqueness of each face, with only the eyes, nose, mouth and ears to work with; history has never repeated a face. This revelation was first presented to her in a talk by Marguerite Wildenhain at the California College of Arts and Crafts before the casting began. What appealed to Asawa was that she and the model with a simple technique, produced something that had nothing to do with "art expressions," capturing a moment, never to return or to be repeated with the passing of time, an experience that precedes the formalization called 'art'."

In citing Asawa's commitment to work that had "nothing to do with 'art expressions,'" Nordland underscores what distinguishes Asawa's art from that of her contemporaries, including the Minimalists.

Asawa's life masks are not portraits in the way that society has come to define that word. They do something unexpected, which is almost the opposite of what most portraits do; they preserve a moment when the subject's eyes are closed and their face is relaxed, but they are not asleep. The pose acknowledges mortality. Asawa recognized that portrait painting and busts give the illusion that one can step away from time's vagaries and that they reflect the social milieu the subject inhabited. Asawa wanted to separate the portrait from the social and from what she called "art expressions," the moment of posing. More important, she wanted to acknowledge that time is unrepeatable and that nothing is permanent. Asawa's understanding of continuous change and time passing is fundamentally different from that which dominates Western art.

Seeing these faces, we know nothing of the individual's social standing. We see the life mask of someone at rest. It could also be—but most definitely isn't—a death mask. And yet, it is as if Asawa's masks were harbingers of the unavoidable future.

This is one of the tensions running throughout all the fired-clay masks that Asawa made between 1966 and 2000. Her work memorializes a brief moment in an individual's life, when he or she was lying on Asawa's kitchen table or a classroom floor. By choosing to use different kinds of clay, which resulted in a wide range of tones—from white and sand to dark brown and nearly black—when fired, Asawa acknowledges racial and ethnic diversity, which is certainly evident in her subjects.

At the same time, Asawa makes no attempt to align actual skin tone with the clay's color, which I think is important to keep in mind. When we look at a group of her masks, do we think about the color of the subject? Without foregrounding this question in her masks, she does ask us how we see a person. Do we see color before a face? What does it mean to see someone face-to-face, as the saying goes?

Asawa essentially removed all the markers we associate with portraits—whether in painting or sculpture—that enable us to recognize and assess someone else. We have only the front of someone's face and hairline. Since the eyes are closed, we cannot—as the ancient Greeks believed—see into the person's soul. What we encounter is someone's unique materiality, as embodied by the attention that Asawa pays to eyebrows, eyelashes, and even the wrinkles in the skin. Nothing about the individual is idealized, improved, or altered. In this, Asawa exposes something fundamental; that each of us is a unique being living in time. In making more than one cast of the same person—as she did with family members—Asawa underscores that person's passage through time.

This is why I think Asawa did not glaze many masks, cover them with a protective coating, or paint them. By low firing the clay, she made masks that radiate vulnerability and fragility; there is nothing protecting them, nothing making the skin of the piece seem impermeable. Everything comes out of her process and choice of materials, what she does and doesn't do to them. This awareness of time passing, and that we cannot escape it, is what her wire sculptures and life masks share.

In her globular looped-wire sculptures hanging down from the ceiling, viewers often see the interplay of shadow and light on a nearby wall. They are sensitive to the ambient circumstances of their placement and the kind of light used to illuminate the room or gallery. These are also not aesthetic bastions claiming to be impervious to time. From dissolving the social hierarchy between individuals to rendering the distinction between abstraction and figuration irrelevant, Asawa's work conveys its deeply radical nature, both aesthetically and politically—as if the two were ever separate.

Richard Hunt's Indisputable Achievement

THE SCULPTOR RICHARD Hunt's career began auspiciously in 1955. Born in Chicago in 1935, he was just nineteen years old when his work was included in the Art Institute of Chicago's Fifty-Eighth Annual Exhibition by Artists of Chicago and Vicinity. Over the next two decades, Hunt's ever-upward trajectory and widening sphere seemed almost certain to guarantee him national and international fame, especially after a survey exhibition of his sculptures opened at New York's Museum of Modern Art in 1971. With that show, Hunt became the first African American sculptor to be showcased by MoMA, more than thirty-five years before the next, Martin Puryear (b. 1941), was given a retrospective in 2007–08. And yet Hunt seems almost unknown outside Chicago. This disjuncture between Hunt's strong local reputation and the almost complete absence of national attention—particularly in what is broadly defined as the art world (galleries, museums, and art magazines)—is, I believe, rooted in a narrow vision of what passes for avant-garde art. In Hunt's case, that narrow vision has relegated his work, once perceived as radical, to the category of "conservative" or even "inconsequential."

To grasp the nature of this repositioning, which started in the 1960s and rapidly accelerated during the 1970s, and the rise of Minimalism, Land Art, and Conceptual Art, I would like to briefly examine Hunt's early career, beginning with the year his work was first recognized. William S. Lieberman, a curator at MoMA, who was visiting the Art Institute of Chicago at the time of the 1955 exhibition, purchased a Hunt sculpture for his personal collection. The New York art dealer Charles Alan also bought one after seeing it in Chicago. A short while later, Hunt signed a contract with Alan, who promised the young sculptor a solo show in New York, which took place in the fall of 1958. In 1956, he won the prestigious Mr. and Mrs. Frank Logan Prize from the Art Institute of Chicago for his sculpture *Construction D*. In 1957, the legendary MoMA curator Dorothy C. Miller—the first to exhibit Isamu Noguchi, Frank Stella, Jasper Johns, Jay DeFeo, and Lee Bontecou in a museum context—obtained a Hunt sculpture for the Museum of Modern Art, before the artist had turned twenty-one years old. *Arachne* (1956) was the first work of his to enter the museum's collection. [1]

In 1961, at the sixty-fourth American Exhibition of Painting and Sculpture, also held at the Art Institute of Chicago, Hunt was awarded the Logan Prize for the second time, for *Construction with Branching Forms*; he would go on to receive the prize for the third time in 1962. Also in 1962, he won the Walter M. Campana Memorial Prize for *Antique Study after Nike* (1961) at the sixty-fifth iteration of the exhibition. That same year, he received a John Simon Guggenheim Memorial Fellowship.

As might be expected of a young, up-and-coming artist who had received such serious accolades in his hometown, Hunt began to show outside Chicago and to receive invitations to teach as a visiting artist. Within a short period of time, he taught at the Yale School of Art and Architecture in New Haven, Connecticut, and at the Chouinard Art School (now California Institute of the Arts) in Los Angeles. While in LA, he met other Black artists working in the Watts neighborhood, including the sculptor Melvin Edwards. This association underscores Hunt's existence in two separate but not equal art worlds, which were defined by race rather than aesthetics. When Hunt left the West Coast and returned to Chicago, he gave Edwards his anvil.

Sixteen years after he first saw Hunt's sculptures in Chicago, Lieberman organized his 1971 one-person exhibition at MoMA. Hunt was thirty-six years old at the time. The extensive exhibition, *The Sculpture of Richard Hunt*, which contained fifty-five sculptures, eight drawings, and twelve prints, received a glowing review by the conservative critic Hilton Kramer in *The New York Times* (March 24, 1971). In his "Introduction," Lieberman characterized Hunt's work in iron, steel, copper, aluminum, and other metals as "three-dimensional 'space drawings,'" which he saw as extending from a tradition that included Julio González and David Smith.[2]

Given this impressive beginning, I think it is fair to reiterate and amplify my inquiry: why isn't Hunt's name more widely known and celebrated in today's art world?

To begin to answer this question, it is necessary to identify and examine a constellation of overlapping factors, one of which is the socio-historical epoch in which Hunt began to exhibit. Hunt's retrospective at MoMA arrived in the aftermath of the Civil Rights Movement; waves of urban unrest, including the Watts Uprising of August 1965; and the 1968 assassination of Martin Luther King, Jr. Pushed by these events, the art world seems to have opened its eyes to African American artists, including those whose practice was largely abstract, for about five years.

The painter Al Loving had a solo show at the Whitney Museum of American Art, New York, in 1969; in 1970, Melvin Edwards—whom Hunt had befriended when he was teaching in Los Angeles—became the first African American sculptor to have a show there; and in 1972, Alma W. Thomas became the first African American woman to be recognized with a solo show at the Whitney. Things seemed to be changing, but for at least two reasons the doors closed once more, particularly for those Black artists who did not make trenchant Black subject matter their focus. One reason is the rise of the Black Arts Movement, which started in 1965 when poet Amiri Baraka (LeRoi Jones) established the Black Arts Repertory Theater in Harlem, New York. The rise of the Black Arts Movement, with its emphasis on Black experience and America's racist history, coincided with the rise of Minimalism and the formalist assertion that one's art was not influenced by one's race, ethnicity, gender, or sexual orientation. Largely rejecting abstract art, the Black Arts Movement emphasized the importance of narrative and storytelling while white critics and artists such as Clement Greenberg and Donald Judd ignored the possibility that anything but purely formal issues was important to art. Ironically, just as Hunt was achieving attention in New York, the doors were closing. Once we recognize the foundation of thinking and experience from which Hunt's sculptures developed, it becomes clear why his work is not better known in the art world.

One of Richard Hunt's many public commissions is located in New York's Harlem neighborhood, at the intersection of Morningside Avenue and West 125th Street. Made of welded and polished bronze, *Harlem Hybrid* (1976) is a rejection of the purity, essentialism, and literalism sought by the artist's contemporaries. If we think of what Carl Andre, Anthony Caro, or Richard Serra were doing throughout the 1970s, it is evident that Hunt was pursuing a different possibility—one that was not geometric, reductive, or purely formal.

As the title of his Harlem sculpture makes clear, Hunt was interested in hybrid forms, in attaining what he called a "synthesis of organic and industrial subject matter." The artist's rejection of pure form, shorn of allusions, particularly interests me. I wonder whether we can see it better now, when the art world seems to be more open to crossing boundaries and reexamining its history of oversights and exclusions.[3]

Made at the beginning of the decade, *Hybrid Form #3* (1970) seems to typify one of Hunt's preoccupations. The vertical, freestanding sculpture begins as a four-sided cast-bronze column that gradually tapers upward before—less than halfway up—transforming into a frozen, liquid-like form that rises farther into the air. A thick, rounded appendage extends from the column, which splits and then divides again into two hornlike projections. Hunt's ascending organic form reminds us that bronze can be either solid (the tapering column) or, when heated, liquid (the rising, undulant form). And the transformation from solid to liquid is what the sculptor both initiates and manipulates. The sculpture's evocation of liquid can be read as signaling a state of constant change.

As I see it, in *Hybrid Form #3*, Hunt is as true to his materials and processes as Richard Serra was when he began rolling and folding thin sheets of lead in 1969. At the same time, I believe that Hunt, in his departures from the work of his contemporaries, inhabits a domain that recognizes and celebrates its own histories and legacies. *Hybrid Form #3* deliberately echoes the familiar presentation of a sculpture as an object mounted on a pedestal. However, instead of culminating in a static or heroic figure at the top, the form changes its very identity as it ascends. In contrast to Frank Stella, who stated in his 1966 interview with Bruce Glaser, "What you see is what you see," Hunt has never allowed his work to become literal, nor has he aligned himself with anti-illusionistic aesthetics. For him, bronze is not just bronze. The challenge is how to be true to his material's identity while making it resonate beyond itself.[4]

Hunt's interest in movement and transformation was influenced by the work of the Italian Futurist painter and sculptor Umberto Boccioni (1882–1916), which he first examined close-up when Boccioni's *Unique Forms of Continuity in Space* (1913) was included in the traveling survey exhibition *Sculpture of the Twentieth Century*, presented at the Art Institute of Chicago in 1953. Ten years after this first encounter with Boccioni—at a time when he was moving beyond "drawing in space" to creating volumetric forms—Hunt made *Antique Study after Boccioni* (1963) in welded steel. In this work, with its embrace of both early modernism and the classical past, Hunt clearly defined a very different path for himself from the one that would be outlined by Judd in his influential essay-manifesto "Specific Objects" (1965), which introduced the idea of an art that was "neither painting nor sculpture."

In the catalogue published on the occasion of Hunt's 1971 exhibition at MoMA, Lieberman made the following observation about the "hybrid" sculptures:

> In their conception and with their suggestion of velocity and energy, however, they owe more to the few sculptures of Umberto Boccioni than to any specific Hellenistic examples. As Hunt became a master of direct metal techniques and as his forms evolved more directly from his technical experimentations, he began another series somewhat more open and fused in space. He called this series "hybrid figures"; and, in these works, elements derived from the human trunk and limbs interlock with those whose reference is botanical and organic.

In this passage, Lieberman identifies two aspects of Hunt's work that continue to play an important role: "velocity and energy," and the interlocking of human forms with those found in nature, suggesting that the two are inseparable.

While underscoring the relationship of Hunt's works to Boccioni's, Lieberman also claims that they do not extend out of "any specific Hellenistic examples." I don't agree with this because, for one, Hunt had already made a work recalling Hellenistic art, *Antique Study After Nike*; also, a number of the "hybrid" sculptures feature two billowing forms extending from a central, rising form, a configuration that recalls *Winged Victory of Samothrace* (200–190 BCE), also known as *Nike of Samothrace*.

In contrast to the literalism that is synonymous with Minimalist sculpture and Conceptual Art, Hunt makes ambiguous forms that court multiple readings. It is important to note that this is not simply a philosophical departure from a prevailing aesthetic; rather, the roots of Hunt's thinking began in his childhood, with many of his inspirations stemming from his early education in Black history.

In 1947, Hunt attended art classes at the South Side Community Art Center (SSCAC), one of which was taught by the Black artist, writer, and educator Margaret Burroughs (1915–2010). Devoted to Black history and the educating of Black children, Burroughs had helped establish the center in May 1941, when the first lady of the United States, Eleanor Roosevelt, dedicated it. Burroughs also founded, in her apartment, the Ebony Museum of Negro History and Art, which evolved into the DuSable Museum of African American History, now part of the Smithsonian Institution and a fixture of Chicago's cultural scene. A number of works by Hunt are in that museum's collection.

From these early encounters, it becomes clear why Hunt may not have been interested in pursuing the avant-garde ideals espoused by Greenberg, Judd, Krauss, and others, which completely ignored the relevance of African art and Black history. In their view, the appropriation of African art by Pablo Picasso was just another step in the progress toward self-referential purity and the expanded field. But as we can see in the work of the Cuban-born Afro-Chinese artist Wifredo Lam (1902–84), one response to appropriation is reappropriation—a reclaiming of what was taken. It is in such a light that we should look at Hunt's work.[5]

In addition to Hunt's involvement with the SSCAC—where he had his first art show in 1952, while still in high school—he also worked part-time in the experimental zoological laboratory at the University of Chicago. There, for six years, he observed animals, their behavior, and their anatomy firsthand. Not surprisingly, these educational and work experiences were grounded in the Hunt family's aspirational desire to better their status in a society that was largely hostile to them because of their race. When Hunt was a child, his mother took him often to Chicago's free museums, including the Field Museum, where he saw examples of African art. According to Hunt, it was there that he made a connection—which he related to his mother—between an African "brush broom" on display and the broom he used to sweep the yard during summer visits to relatives in Hart County, Georgia.

This anecdote reveals the beginnings of a different approach to art. By learning about Black history and African art, Hunt recognized his own separateness. Rather than focusing on appropriation, rupture, and rejection—what would be the point of rejecting art and art practices that were never yours in the first place?—Hunt concentrated on reappropriation and preservation without becoming nostalgic: How do you make the past new? How do you show its vitality and importance to the present, particularly during the Civil Rights struggle, which, contrary to what many might like to think, has hardly ended?

IN EARLY SCULPTURES by Hunt such as *Wing Bloom* (1957) and *Flight Form* (1958), we see another of the sculptor's preoccupations: flight and birds, winged bodies capable of overcoming gravity. Even as his work changed formally in the late 1960s, becoming more massive than linear, he maintained this interest, a fascination that had been deepened by his experiences at the zoological laboratory.

In *Linear Peregrination* (1963), three tapering chrome rods support a horizontal chrome spine. The definition of "peregrination" is to travel from one place to another, but not in a straight line; Hunt's analogous horizontal form twists and turns and branches out as it passes through space. Could *Linear Peregrination* be an allusion to Hunt's own journey as well as to the history of Black people and Civil Rights in America?

Two years after *Linear Peregrination*, Hunt welded steel rods together to create a linear structure with a birdlike form attached to one of its legs. The work's title, *Peregrine Forms* (1965), marks the first time that Hunt cites a specific avian species from the raptor class (owls, falcons, and hawks).

The peregrine falcon is a bird of prey whose diet consists of medium-sized birds and small mammals. Historically, the art of falconry—the training of raptors to fly and hunt at the behest of humans—goes back as far as ancient Mesopotamia, with the earliest accounts dating to about 2000 BCE. Given its difficulty, the practice of falconry most likely started much earlier, in an age before humankind developed writing. The word "falcon" is related to the Latin *faix*, which means "sickle," a reference to the silhouette of the bird's wings in flight. Might this be one of the inspirations for Hunt's use of curving, sicklelike shapes in his sculptures?

Historical Circle and *Peregrine Section* (1975) are two large sculptures installed in front of Bentley Historical Library at the University of Michigan in Ann Arbor. Hunt made the works after he started working with COR-TEN steel, at a time when public commissions were becoming an important part of his practice. The three relatively flat, curving shapes rising out of *Peregrine Section*, particularly the form in the center, suggest the stance and anatomy of birds.

Hunt's references to falcons and falconry anticipate Martin Puryear's *On the Tundra* (1986) and *Untitled (Falcon)* (1986–87). And yet, as far as I can tell, no one has commented on the interest in nature and Black history shared by these two prominent Black sculptors, who were born six years apart but are associated with different generations. By overlooking connections such as this, art historians fail to recognize the linkages among Black artists working abstractly; to obtain a more complete history of modern art, it is incumbent upon us to trace them.

SHORTLY AFTER HUNT finished *Harlem Hybrid* (1976), he had a large two-part sculpture, *Jacob's Ladder* (1977), installed in the atrium of the Carter G. Woodson Regional Library on the Southside of Chicago. Built in 1975, and expanded in 1998, the Woodson Library is the repository for the Vivian G. Harsh Research Collection of Afro-American History and Literature, which is the largest collection of its kind in the Midwest. The rolling bronze ladder, which hangs down directly above a piece Hunt has set on the floor, is connected to two horizontal bars stretching between the two vertical forms that extend down from one of the two larger forms attached to the building's structural I beams.

In the biblical book of Genesis, Jacob has a dream while fleeing his brother, Esau. In the dream, he sees a ladder that is set upon the earth but reaches heaven, with angels "ascending and descending" upon it. Jacob has the dream while sleeping with his head on a stone. In *Jacob's Ladder*, Hunt restated this narrative in abstract forms. Set inside a library, the suspended ladder and evocation of a dreaming mind gain still more meanings, as the gap between what is on the floor and what extends down from the building's I beams brings together a visceral response with a symbolic reading.

Nearly forty years later, Hunt's *Swing Low* (2016), a bronze sculpture of flat, rippling shapes, was suspended from the ceiling in the main lobby of the new National Museum of African American History and Culture in Washington, DC. The sculpture's title alludes to the nineteenth-century African American spiritual "Swing Low, Sweet Chariot." Formally, Hunt's sculpture is made of arcing shapes and winglike forms, which echo the sculpture's swinging movement as well as being lifted up. Simultaneously site-specific and culturally specific, both *Jacob's Ladder* and *Swing Low* deal with the subject of deliverance from tyranny and slavery. And yet, I cannot imagine Judd or Krauss being moved to write about these works, or Hunt's sculptures in general, because they and their associates would have considered them irrelevant to art's progress toward the expanded field. They would not have seen Hunt's use of suspended forms within a specific architectural setting as innovative.

Whether creating organic forms that rise from columnar bases or stacking airy clusters of winglike shapes, Hunt is speaking to the ideals of transformation and aspiration. His work springs from motivations beyond the art world's obeisance to the ideas of rejection and rupture, which it still considers an integral feature of the avant-garde. The history of Black people in the United States of America, no one needs to be reminded, has been constantly marked by rejection and rupture. Thus, in his art, from the outset, Hunt has focused on alternative possibilities. It is time that we honor his vision.

The Unseen Professors

(on Leo Amino, Minoru Niizuma, and John Pai)

THIS ESSAY FOCUSES on the work of Leo Amino (1911–89), Minoru Niizuma (1930–98), and John Pai (b. 1937), three Asian sculptors who were born between 1911 and 1937 in Taiwan, Japan, and Korea, respectively, and immigrated to America. Eventually, all of them moved to New York City, where they worked and taught for many years in prestigious art programs. Despite being members of different generations, their teaching careers overlapped for more than a decade (1965–77), during which time a generation of artists associated with Minimalism and site-specific art gained much of the art world's attention. By reexamining this period through significant works by Amino, Niizuma, and Pai, this essay will highlight the accomplishments of three independent Asian American artists who were neither associated with a mainstream movement or style nor ever fully accepted by the art world, despite showing in prestigious New York venues, such as the Whitney Museum of American Art, the Metropolitan Museum of Art, and the Museum of Modern Art.

Equally important is that the work and material choices made by these Asian American artists have almost nothing in common with each other's. Employing distinct processes, they rigorously pursued their own trajectories, never attempting to align themselves with the dominant currents of the art world. The refusal to embrace mainstream thinking may have been due partly to their realization that they would always be regarded as outsiders or outliers. This grasp of their problematic status in relationship to the dominant art world and its deeply embedded strain of inherent prejudices was first hinted at in 1997, when Amino, Niizuma, and Pai were shown together, along with other Asian American artists, in the exhibition *Asian Traditions/Modern Expressions: Asian American Artists and Abstraction, 1945–1970*, organized by Jeffrey Wechsler for the Jane Voorhees Zimmerli Art Museum at Rutgers University (1997). However, in contrast to that exhibition, which largely focused on Asian American painters and their relationship to abstraction, particularly gestural painting and the development of Abstract Expressionism, this essay centers on the relationship of three innovative sculptors and the alternative bodies of work they developed in the face of Minimalism and the dominant paradigm of avant-garde art that was developed by Donald Judd and Rosalind Krauss starting in the mid-1960s.

In the early 1960s, when mainstream art critics of color were nonexistent in the American art world, much critical discussion revolved around the "death of painting," forecast by the rise of Andy Warhol and the use of silkscreen and other forms of mechanical reproduction. As the art world's attention continued to shift away from painting throughout the 1960s and ultimately focused on Conceptual Art and other non-painting practices in the 1970s, a parallel "death of sculpture" began to gather momentum in New York around the mid-1960s. Influenced by painting's fallen status and the rejection of the handmade in favor of the machine-tooled object and modular forms, a generation of sculptors began to rely on industrial fabrication for the production of their work, while others incorporated store-bought objects into their sculptures. Working with fabricators or incorporating ready-mades into their work, artists such as Donald Judd, Dan Flavin, and Carl Andre began to receive critical acclaim for a cool and reductive hands-off approach that was soon designated by the term Minimalism, which was seen as supplanting the work of David Smith, Mark di Suvero, and sculptors who worked directly in wood and stone.

In his essay "Specific Objects" (1965), Donald Judd theorized, contextualized, and underscored why a change in approach and materials was historically unavoidable. Writing about sculpture, Judd states: "So far the most obvious difference within this diverse work is between that which is something of an object, a single thing, and that which is open and extended, more or less environmental." In 1979, nearly fifteen years after Judd's essay was published, the artist historian Rosalind Krauss published "Sculpture in the Expanded Field" in *October*. In this essay, which Krauss later developed into a book, she elaborated upon Judd's idea of the "environmental" by applying a precise diagram to define the structural parameters of sculpture, architecture, and landscape art. Since their publication, Judd's and Krauss's essays have achieved canonical status, influencing the way sculpture is received, discussed, and evaluated. Although they were written fourteen years apart, what they have in common is a rejection of sculpture as a handmade object and as a "single thing" in favor of works of art that are fabricated and "environmental." While the authority of these texts has seldom been challenged, and their dominance has been evident, I want to offer another way of reading them.[1]

Aligning themselves with the avant-garde tradition, which is based on a belief in art's progress toward pure presence, both Judd and Krauss make aesthetic arguments rooted in the color-blind thinking associated with various Western philosophies, be it Plato, Immanuel Kant, or French post-structuralist theory. Although I don't presume any venomous design, neither "Specific Objects" nor "Sculpture in the Expanded Field" mentions a single artist of color, except as an aside or afterthought, which is in keeping with the avant-garde tradition as it developed in America during the latter half of the twentieth century, in the aftermath of what Irving Sandler defined as "the triumph" of American art. Further, to suppose that Judd's and Krauss's texts trace the only routes of advanced thinking for artists to take is to believe that everyone is born into the same culture and subscribes to the same avant-garde tradition, which we know is patently untrue. If, as Judd argues in his essay, "the disinterest in painting and sculpture is a disinterest in doing it again," then the identity of the person who decides the meaning of "doing it again" is the key here, isn't it?[2]

Like Judd, Krauss emphasizes rupture. Their shared belief in the importance of bursting away from the past, coupled with a focus on form, material, and process, ignores certain crucial issues, such as the historical and social circumstances the individual is born into, and the role that one's culture, race, upbringing, gender identity, and sexual orientation might play in the making of art. I am not arguing for an autobiographical or diary-like approach or even an "I" centered transparency. Rather, I am stating that the ideals proposed by Judd and Krauss efface the sociological aspects of the individual to such an extreme degree that it approaches Warhol's goal of being machinelike, which is a way of denying racial difference and suppressing cultural and gender difference and the role they might play in the making of art. By doing so, Judd and Krauss fail to recognize their resistance to acknowledging race and culture as an important feature in the production of art, as well as deny their own complicity with an aesthetics that shares something with colonialist-imperialist thinking and the so-called "triumph" of American art.

If we further examine Judd's "disinterest in doing it again," we are compelled to ask why he never acknowledged Leo Amino, who began using polyester resin (plastic) around the end of World War II, and had work in all but two Whitney Annuals for sculpture (the precursor to the Whitney Biennial) between 1947 and 1962. It is unlikely that Judd was unaware of Amino's work, as they both had work in the 1965 group show *Plastics*, which the Conceptual Artist Dan Graham organized at the now legendary John Daniels Gallery that he opened and ran from 1964 to 1965. It was in *Plastics* that Amino debuted his cast resin pieces collectively titled *Refractionals*. Five years later, in 1970, Amino's work was included in the large touring group show *A Plastic Presence*, which was organized by Tracy Atkinson, director of the Milwaukee Art Center. *A Plastic Presence* opened at the Jewish Museum

(1969-1970) in New York and after traveling to the Milwaukee Art Center (1970) concluded its tour at the San Francisco Museum of Art (1970). Along with Amino, the exhibition of nearly fifty artists included work by Richard Artschwager, Eva Hesse, Craig Kauffman, Helen Pashgian, and Richard Van Buren.

In her discussion of the intersection of sculpture, architecture, and landscape art, Krauss never mentions Isamu Noguchi, who was commissioned by Marcel Breuer to design a Japanese garden adjacent to UNESCO's headquarters in Paris in 1957. One likely reason for Krauss's rejection is that Noguchi's site-specific installation did not sufficiently conform to her aesthetics to rank consideration. By her standards, a Japanese garden was neither American nor avant-garde enough. By insisting that their views are the only viable measures that can be used to assess a work of art, Judd and Krauss appoint themselves gatekeepers to a community of individuals who deny the existence of those who do not subscribe to their ideologies. It is against this backdrop that Amino, Niizuma, and Pai made their work. In their invisibility in the art world and erasure from art history, they share something with other artists of Asian descent, such as Wifredo Lam, Isamu Noguchi, and Ruth Asawa, who exhibited their work in America but did not go on to become celebrities (like Yayoi Kusama and Yoko Ono).

We know that in Volume II of *"Primitivism" in 20th Century Art: Affinity of the Tribal and the Modern* (1984, edited by William S. Rubin), published well after Amino, Pai, and Niizuma began working in New York, Evan Maurer, in his essay, "Dada and Surrealism," describes Lam this way:

> This was [Wifredo] Lam's greatest synthesis as a Surrealist: He combined a close contact with tribal rituals with the cultural and artistic sophistication of a Western intellectual.

Maurer's "close contact" suggests that there is no autobiographical connection between the artist and "tribal rituals"; it certainly does not convey that he participated in these religious practices as a child. The facts that Lam's godmother, Mantønica Wilson, was a Yoruba priestess, and that he formed a lasting relationship with the Black Martinican poet Aimé Césaire, one of the founders of the Négritude movement, are considered irrelevant by Rubin and Maurer. Rather, Lam possessed the "cultural and artistic sophistication of a Western intellectual," which is code for passing as white. Nothing about Lam's racial and cultural background is considered worthy of consideration. It is within this situation of invisibility and suppression based on hierarchical thinking that Amino, Niizuma, and Pai lived and made their work.

LEO AMINO WAS born in Taiwan in 1911 and grew up in Tokyo, Japan. In 1929, he immigrated to the United States, where he lived south of San Francisco, studying for two years at San Mateo Junior College. He then moved to New York, where he studied briefly at NYU. After dropping out, he remained in New York and began working for a Japanese wood importing firm and taking home ebony samples to carve. Although Amino had no formal art training, he grew increasingly interested in sculpture. In 1937, he studied briefly at the American Artists School with Chaim Gross, a leading proponent of direct carving. In 1938, Amino traveled to England, where he saw the work of Henry Moore and Moore's use of pierced volumes. In 1939, Amino and Isamu Noguchi were paired in an exhibition at the World's Fair in New York. In 1940 he had his first solo exhibition at the cooperative Artists Gallery, where Josef Albers and Ad Reinhardt also showed. It is where Albers first learned of Amino's work, and because of that introduction would later invite him to teach at Black Mountain College.

On December 12, 1941, Amino and six other artists of Japanese descent who were living in New York penned and signed a letter expressing their shock at the bombing of Pearl Harbor on December 7, declaring they were ready to "bear arms if necessary to insure the final victory for the democratic forces of the World." During World War II, while translating for the United States Navy, he became interested in the sculptural possibilities of polyester resin (or plastic) after it was declassified by the military, and he began casting it in 1948, long before artists such as DeWain Valentine and Rockne Krebs began (and became known for) using resin in their work.

Looking back at Amino's career from when he first carved wood in the early 1930s and in the late '40s began casting, it seems to me that he was engaged with issues of form, from totems and vertical structures to transparency, color, and light (which might have been inspired by his contact with Albers and Bauhaus thinking). Working with two radically different materials (wood and plastic), which he at times combined, and employing two different processes (carving and casting), while focusing on form, light, color, and transparency without making any overt reference to being Asian did not gain Amino a larger circle of attention. As with other artists of color working in America in the twentieth century, there was a barrier he could not break through.

In addition to inviting Amino to teach at Black Mountain (summer 1946 and 1950), Albers helped secure him a position at Cooper Union, where he taught from 1952 until 1977, despite having no formal education or college degree, and where he introduced his student Jack Whitten to direct carving. Albers, who left Germany with his wife Anni in 1933, when the Nazis closed the Bauhaus, was an instrumental figure in Amino's life, more so than any other American artist. In addition to inviting Amino to teach, Albers invited Jacob Lawrence and Gwendolyn Knight Lawrence to teach at Black Mountain College in 1946, a few years after the school began to incorporate African American culture and history into its programming. In order to protect the Lawrences from the world of Jim Crow and institutionally sanctioned racism, especially below the Mason-Dixon Line, Albers got the school to provide private transportation to bring them to the campus, which they did not leave during their residency. The rest of America did not mirror Albers's open embrace of artists of color.

In addition to being included in many Whitney Annuals, Amino had work in other important group shows, including *Carv-*

ers-Modelers-Welders (1950) at the Museum of Modern Art, New York, and *American Sculpture* (1951) at the Metropolitan Museum of Art, New York, and he was one of six sculptors who had work in *The New Decade: 35 American Painters and Sculptors* (1955) at the Whitney Museum of American Art.

As I cited earlier, in 1965, Dan Graham put on the exhibition *Plastics* (1965) at John Daniels Gallery. In 1969, Vito Acconci wrote this about Amino's resin works in *ARTnews*:

> The over-all form looks solid, holding the viewer away from it, while the inside is elusive and tempts the viewer in. Seen from one direction, there is an agglomeration of color, while, seen from another, the color almost disappears; the viewer enters it unconsciously.[3]

It is clear from Acconci's description that the views of Amino's resin works change, and this is caused by the side you are looking at. This is just one of the many experiential conditions that Amino attained in his work, particularly the *Refractionals*.

I have cited these events in Amino's career because they convey something of the gap between having your work seen and having it recognized, in his case, for its innovative use of materials. Both Graham and Acconci called attention to Amino's resin works, but these instances did not lead to a larger recognition. This means that Amino's work was seen, but remained under the radar, and that he was regarded as a largely invisible or peripheral presence. After his death in 1989, his work was not exhibited in a New York gallery for thirty years. It is this condition of near invisibility that Niizuma and Pai, who were born two decades or more after Amino, entered into when they began teaching in New York.

MINORU NIIZUMA WAS born in Tokyo in 1930 and graduated from Tokyo National University of Fine Arts and Music in 1955. In order to make modern art in a society that provided little institutional support and had few galleries, Niizuma became a member of an artist-run group in Tokyo, the Modern Art Association (1954–58). He was elected a permanent jury member in 1957. During this time, he taught sculpture and drawing at Seijo School, Tokyo (1955–58), and his work began to gain attention. In 1956, he was awarded a commission for a public monument by the city of Tokyo and in 1958 by the Tokyo Asia Center. Shortly after, realizing that there were no real opportunities to exhibit other than the group shows organized by the Modern Art Association and other artist-run groups, Niizuma immigrated to New York in 1959.

It seems that it took some years for Niizuma to get his footing. He worked as an instructor at the Brooklyn Museum Art School (1964–70). In addition to teaching and making sculpture, he photographed Yoko Ono's performances, such as the legendary *Cut Piece* (1964), performed at the Carnegie Recital Hall on March 21, 1965. The photographs that Niizuma took of Ono's performances from the 1960s to the early '70s—often the only record—are considered iconic and have been reproduced many times.

In 1966, Niizuma had his first solo show in New York at Howard Wise Gallery. His work was included in two Whitney Annuals (1966 and 1968). In 1966, he was one of forty-six artists whose work was included in *The New Japanese Painting and Sculpture* at the Museum of Modern Art, organized by Dorothy Miller and William S. Lieberman, and in the early 1970s he showed with Gimpel and Weitzenhoffer. Despite exhibiting in New York and being included in museum shows, Niizuma attained greater recognition outside of America. In 1976, he had a retrospective at the Seibu Museum of Art in Tokyo and a decade later, in 1986, at the Gulbenkian Museum in Lisbon, Portugal.

In his review in the *New York Times* (April 15, 1972), the conservative critic John Canaday stated: "Mr. Niizuma has two loves, marble and the abstract patterns of traditional Japanese art. He makes the most of both by cutting and polishing his stones to reveal grains and colors in shapes that echo the patterns of folk art, fabrics and ritual vessels." While Canaday sees a connection between Niizuma's Japanese heritage and his sculptures, he also isolates him from Western art, implicitly suggesting that the work is solely Japanese. This reductive review does not recognize what Niizuma got from Western art, particularly Minimalism and its reliance on geometric forms and the use of repetition. This is not particularly surprising, but it does reveal some of the inherent prejudices that Niizuma faced in America, which was still celebrating the "triumph" of American art.

That Niizuma carved in stone further isolated him from the commercial New York art world, which, under the influence of Pop Art and Minimalism, had pivoted away from the handmade and began focusing almost exclusively on works that involved fabrication, modular repetition, and the use of commercially available objects. If the work could not be made by others or assembled from obtainable things, it was considered traditional because it did not break with a Western notion of the past. And yet, Niizuma's work and the philosophy informing it can be seen as both a break with Japanese traditional art and an implicit critique of Western materialism and the belief in timelessness and art's permanent status.

In works such as *Unknown (Water in the Mountain Adjacent)* (n.d.), *Water Fall* (ca. 1986), and *Unknown (Water Fall Adjacent)* (ca. 1986), Niizuma explores his longstanding interest in states of constant change, as signified by waterfalls and rivers. This was not an abstract concept to Niizuma, who had worked as a fisherman in Hokkaido, Japan's northernmost prefecture, when he was a young man. No doubt, he was also familiar with the archetypal motif in East Asian art of a scholar contemplating a waterfall, which was regarded as an emblematic sign of change and dissipation. By working in stone, Niizuma effectively dislodges a motif common to ink painting and the pictorial world, and introduces it into the domain of sculpture and the three-dimensional. Whereas the painter can use a brush to depict the scholar contemplating the waterfall, Niizuma had to find a way to address in stone this phenomenon of constant change without becoming pictorial. This is what is new about Niizuma's sculptures, and why it is wrong to regard him as a traditional artist because he carved directly in stone.

In Niizuma's sculptures, the elements and forces of water (liquid), descending forms (gravity), and destruction (water crashing against stone) become stone and stillness, polished finish and rough surface. Viewers might even find themselves asking, what forces made this work? Was it water that polished these stones just as it has smoothed the glass found at the beach? Or did crashing water break this piece, leaving different surfaces jagged? Niizuma's recognition of nature's power is fundamentally different from the attitudes common to the Minimalists, who believe they can impose a permanent form on nature but seldom recognize its power in their work.

This is how Sakai Tadayasu described the tension between smooth and rough in Niizuma's work:

> It is not so much that the work has been abandoned in an unfinished state but that an uncanny contrast has been created between the sharply chiseled areas which are seemingly caressed to a polish and areas that remain in their rough, untouched state.[4]

This is one of the contrasts found in Niizuma's work. Others can be seen in works such as *Water Fall* and *Unknown (Water Fall Adjacent)* (both ca. 1986), in which the artist establishes an interplay between the stone's blue veining and the shape and interaction of the cut pieces. This is another one of Niizuma's innovations, which I think was not recognized in America. Canaday got a trace of it, but I don't think he fully grasped what the sculptor was up to, and he did not pursue it further in his writing, nor did anyone else.

In the beginning of the 1980s, Niizuma started working in Portugal. During this decade, he helped form a link between Portugal and Japan. This included bringing Japanese art to Portugal and introducing Portuguese artists to Japan. One reason he was attracted to working in Portugal was the marble and other stones that he discovered were available.

In *Castle of the Eye III* (n.d.), which Niizuma carved from pure white Portuguese marble, the four facing surfaces are identically marked by physically receding, incrementally smaller nesting rectangles whose parameters are established by the previous rectangle. The shallow, physically receding space pulls the viewer in, but does not permit entry to the interior. The first *Castle of the Eye* (1964), which employs repetition without relying on fabrication, is in the collection of the Museum of Modern Art, and should be paired with one of Judd's boxes in an exhibition. Do we want to contemplate the material surface of Niizuma's marble or the way Judd reproduced the industrial world of color and material in art? I am not of the mind that there is only one way. Do we want a work marked by the artist's repetitive but changing labor or a smooth, shiny, timeless presence? What is the dialogue that works by Niizuma and Judd would have with each other if placed in the same room? Is it a one-sided conversation? I don't see it that way.

Widely appreciated in Portugal, thirty pieces were installed in the Minoru Niizuma Sculpture Garden, which the collector and patron José Berardo established next to his Bacalhoa Winery-Museum. I believe that the attention and accolades that Niizuma received during his life, mostly in Portugal and Japan, and the current invisibility of his work in America, where he lived and worked for nearly forty years, suggest that we give his work another look.

In his sculptures, Niizuma often juxtaposes a polished surface with a rough, pitted area. In contrast to the Western tradition, as epitomized by Constantin Brancusi's complete control over a stone, resulting in an embodiment of perfected essence and "timelessness," Niizuma acknowledged time's inescapable effects. By having the outer edges of *Unknown* (black marble, 1982) rough, he anticipates the ultimate effects of time. Is *Unknown*—with a hole piercing each of the kitty-corner sides—complete or broken off from something larger that we cannot see, even in our mind's eye? This recognition of fragmentation and erosion stands in contrast to the impeccable Minimalist works by Judd, the stainless steel geometries of David Smith, and the COR-TEN steel totems of Beverly Pepper. It is in his synthesis of geometric forms such as a cube or a pyramid that one sees the influence of Minimalism. However, by presenting the split or broken halves of a highly polished form, Niizuma recognizes that nothing is impervious to time, not even a work of art, and that it is an illusion to think otherwise. In this regard, he believed that art was part of life, rather than separate from it, and that any gesture toward permanence was doomed.

In other works, Niizuma's carving transforms a solid column of stone into fluid surfaces, suggesting that change is also inescapable, and that marble—that sign of empire and permanence—is not a bulwark against time. This is the opposite of Western thinking, and one of Niizuma's great accomplishments; he transforms stone into something both unblemished and broken, impervious and vulnerable, as well as brings the pictorial possibilities of veining into play. He underscores that the cycle of time we live in is far vaster and more powerful than we can imagine.

JOHN PAI WAS born in Seoul, Korea, in 1937, the youngest of three children. His father, an activist Korean Presbyterian minister committed to Korean liberation, was often away, and Pai did not meet him until the end of World War II, when he was eight. His mother, who spent her childhood in Russia, where she received her education, and which she and her family were forced to leave during the Russian Civil War (1917–22), raised him and his older siblings. During World War II and the Japanese occupation his mother brought the children to Ilsan, a rural area northwest of Seoul. Because of his parents' political leanings, Pai and his family were isolated from other Korean families, and he spent much of his time alone, as he was much younger than his brother and sister. Pai began to draw at an early age, and his mother taught him to play the piano. When he was eight, his mother arranged for him to study art with a man who had received French academic training.

In 1949, shortly after North and South Korea became formally separate countries, Pai's family traveled to America and, because of his father's religious affiliations, they ended up in Wheeling,

West Virginia. On the way to Wheeling, they stopped in Toledo, Ohio, and spent a night with a family that Pai's father knew. When his father was told that his children should have American names, he announced that his youngest son and daughter would be called John and Mary. When Pai was fifteen, his parents returned to Korea, and he began living with an American family in Wheeling. By this time, his brother and sister were on their own, trying to start their lives in a new country.

During a series of interviews with Leyla Vural in the summer of 2021, Pai said that while in Wheeling, he soon became involved with sports, particularly football, as he saw it as a way to belong to a group as well as demonstrate his athleticism in a contact sport. It was also at this time that Pai, who had been going to Saturday art classes, had his first solo exhibition at the Oglebay Institute in Wheeling. Six years later, at the age of twenty-one, he received a full scholarship to attend Pratt Institute, and moved to New York, where he lived with his sister and studied industrial design. Two years later, in 1960, inspired by the steel sculptures of Theodore Roszak, which he had seen in the exhibition *New Images of Man* at the Museum of Modern Art, he called Roszak up and eventually began working as his studio assistant as well as helping him install a show at the Pierre Matisse Gallery. Deeply affected by the war and the Holocaust, the Polish-born Roszak began working with welded metals after the end of World War II. In an email he sent to me in 2019, Pai described Roszak as "patient and caring," and he believes his time working for him accelerated his education, especially with materials.

In 1962, Pai graduated from Pratt with a BFA in industrial design, and two years later, he got an MFA in sculpture there. In 1965, he became the youngest professor to start teaching at Pratt and was appointed head of the sculpture department. This means that within a period of three years, Pai went from being an undergraduate to a professor assigned to direct a department.

During the mid-1960s, as he was starting his teaching career at Pratt, Pai got married, bought a carriage house in the Clinton Hill area of Brooklyn, and had two children. He and his wife, Eunsook, also began having parties in their home for diasporic Korean artists, musicians, and writers living in New York. This is how he met Nam June Paik, who moved to New York from Germany in 1964, Kim Whanki, a pioneer of abstract painting in Korea, and Kim Tschang-Yeul, who became known for his waterdrop paintings after he moved to Paris in 1969. Pai recounted to me that although he and Paik never talked about their art, he enjoyed singing Korean folk songs while Pai played the piano in his home, joined by others at the party. Although Pai was younger than Whanki, who lived in New York from 1963 until 1974, and Kim Tschang-Yeul, who lived in New York from 1966 to 1969, they were supportive of him and his work. Later, Whanki's widow helped Pai get gallery representation in Korea. Pai, who grew up displaced from his country, was reconnected to it by another Korean. This provided him with an opportunity to show his art.

This group of diasporic Koreans was Pai's community, which existed apart from the mainstream, white art world. It seems to me that this coterie of artists, who knew each other at a crucial point in their careers, has never been acknowledged as an important force in New York. Their encounter with New York art had a different effect on each of them, even as it also inspired them to be more resolute in their pursuit of an art that had little to do with Western popular culture, fabrication, or the use of mechanical reproduction.

Recognizing their roots in Korean culture and a history of striving for liberation—a struggle in which Pai's activist parents played significant roles—Whanki and Tschang-Yeul did not try to assimilate and become Western artists. This attitude is crucial to understanding Pai's sculpture, which does not resemble anything else being made in New York during the 1970s and '80s. In the review "Sculptor John Pai weaves life into wires" by Kwon Meeyoo that appeared in the *Korea Times*, Pai said of his use of steel wire in his sculptures, "Steel wires are affordable and durable, but can disappear after becoming rusty. I like such a nature of wire, because it is similar to that of a living thing."

In the unpublished oral history conducted by Vural, Pai makes a further distinction about his use of steel:

> [David Smith] loved working with heavy pieces of metal. [. . .] So there was a branch of people who liked the idea of working with heavy chunks of metal, geometric, and I think the basic strength of steel. So they wanted steel to look like steel. Whereas I think I was beginning to see the other side of steel, which with a welding torch, you're taking something very strong and solid and you're melting it until it's liquid. So, that's the side that fascinated me, because it seemed to offer an incredible range of flexibility. So from there, I began to experiment with what the torch can do.

In these two statements about steel, one sees that Pai is working out of an aesthetic that is rooted in a different worldview than the ones espoused by Western sculptors, including David Smith, Donald Judd, and Richard Serra, and their collective belief that art can exist as a bastion against time. Pai's recognition of impermanence and liquidity shares little with Smith's placement of steel sculptures in the fields around his house in Bolton Landing, New York, Judd's placement of concrete sculptures in Marfa, Texas, or Serra's *Áfangar (Standing Stones)* on Viðey Island, a national preserve across the harbor from Reykjavík, Iceland. While these artists impose their work on the landscape, Pai is informed by his interest in various branches of science, including physics and biology, and states of change. Given his early intention to study architecture, it seems to me that he has expanded his interest in visible structures to include invisible and theoretical ones. Both Smith and Judd believe in permanence, while Pai and Niizuma have a different understanding of nature, materials, and time.

In 1963, in response to assisting Roszak, he developed a way of making art that has characterized his work ever since. This is how he put it to me in an email after I asked him when he decided to work solely with thin steel rods, which may or may not be copper coated:

> I wanted to reduce the amount of tooling & machining and simplify the process so that it would be more like drawing in space. Reducing the size of the basic unit gave me a lot of freedom.

WORKING WITHIN A strong and visible material constraint of steel wire, Pai's process is slow and incremental, literally attaching one section to another until a form emerges. Many of Pai's pieces consist of open, swirling, and climbing forms made of thin steel rods welded together. The grids seem capable of attaining any contortion, torque, or change in size. He does not do a drawing for these works, and the final outcome is the result of an open-ended process, which he likens to that of a jazz musician. I think it is telling that the composer he most often listens to while working is Bach.

A number of Pai's open, self-contained, freestanding works are composed of a form inside a form inside a form. In the masterful *Involution* (1974), one sees the circular perimeter of an open linear grid rising off the floor until it becomes a plump, vaselike form that is open to investigation. As it rises from the floor, the grid swells out and then curls in until it forms a circular opening at the top. As the opening descends, like a tunnel, into the interior of the outer shell, it becomes a visual, three-dimensional echo of the outer form. Inside this interior form we see a teardrop form rising—a form sits inside a form, which sits inside a larger form, all of which are connected by a flexible grid of lines. *Involution*'s pot-like form evokes a state of continuous change. Instead of imposing the work on the landscape while claiming perfection and permanence, Pai addresses change as a constant in his dynamic structures made of twisting and bending lines and curving and collapsing planes.

Pai's sculptures are not static. Works such as *Involution* seem to be in a state of change; in some cases, it is like a three-dimensional record of a transformation that has been stilled so that we might scrutinize it. We see his forms as well as see through them. They feel solid and vulnerable, sturdy and delicate. Largely eschewing solid forms, Pai's sculptures are precise three-dimensional drawings in space. Working with the simplest, most pared-down means—cut, bent, and welded steel rods—Pai has attained a remarkable fluidity in his work. More than meticulous drawings in space, they are meditations on inescapable change and disruption, topographical models of unseen forces.

In different ways, Amino, Niizuma, and Pai have explored a lifelong concern with change, rather than the desire to make a permanent and timeless monument. It is a distinction worth pondering in light of our continued arrogance toward and degradation of our environment, and just one of many reasons why their work deserves a longer, sustained look.

III.

On Reconsidering Identity in Art

On March 25, 1941, Wifredo Lam sailed from Marseille, France, to Cuba, where he was born. He was the child of a mixed marriage: his mother was Ana Serafina Castilla, whose legacy was Spanish and African, and his father was Enrique Yam-Lam, who was Cantonese. He was returning to a country that he had left nearly twenty years earlier, in 1923, when he sailed to Spain to further his study of art. During his journey home, he and his fellow passengers and friends, such as Andre Breton, were detained in Martinique because the Vichy government regarded them as traitors. It was during this period of detention that he and Breton met the Martinican poet Aimé Césaire, who had written *Cahier d'un retour au pays natal* (*Notebook of a Return to the Native Land*) in 1938. In this book Césaire used the term Négritude, a poetic and theoretical affirmation of African culture as it had manifested itself in the Caribbean. In 1943, Lam provided the illustrations for the Cuban edition, which was translated by Lydia Cabrera. The publication of this signal poem—which was the first and only time that Lam, Césaire, and Cabrera collaborated—introduced the concept of Négritude, a collective identity of Black people living in the diaspora, to Cuba and its Spanish-speaking population.

Césaire was not without his critics. The most important one was Édouard Glissant, a Martinican who was fifteen years Césaire's junior. In the late 1940s, Glissant began formulating an alternative to Césaire's Négritude. The term he came up with was "creolization." Césaire had argued for a Pan-African identity for all people of African descent living in the diaspora, while Glissant believed in a nonhierarchical and local situation in which the children of mixed marriages could construct their own identities. Whereas Césaire believed in a static sense of identity, Glissant believed in a fluid one.

Having written about Lam for the first time in 1988, I was naturally interested in the new exhibition *Lydia Cabrera and Édouard Glissant: Trembling Thinking* at the Americas Society, curated by Hans Ulrich Obrist, Gabriela Rangel, and Asad Raza. Along with early editions of books by Cabrera and Glissant, magazines containing their articles, drawings by Cabrera, and a wonderful film interview with Glissant, the exhibition contains works done in different mediums by Etel Adnan, Kader Attia, Tania Bruguera, Manthia Diawara, Mestre Didi, Melvin Edwards, Simone Fattal, Sylvie Glissant, Koo Jeong A, Wifredo Lam, Marc Latamie, Roberto Matta, Julie Mehretu, Philippe Parreno, Amelia Peláez, Asad Raza, Anri Sala, Antonio Seguí, Diamond Stingily, Elena Tejada-Herrera, Jack Whitten, and Pedro Zylbersztajn. Many of the works—but not all—directly address or deal with Glissant and Cabrera and their considerations of identity.

This is the kind of group exhibition that rarely happens in New York—a gathering of artists from different countries, cultures, generations, and aesthetic approaches focused on the issues surrounding the construction of identity. And while one could quibble about aspects of the show, including the dearth of context provided by the wall text, there was a lot of material to see and think about. If one purpose of a group exhibition is to inspire viewers to learn more about the different artists and writers they have encountered, then this show more than succeeded.

In the jointly written catalog essay, "Trembling Thinking, or Ethnography of the Unknowable," the curators state:

> For Cabrera and Glissant, thinking beyond narrow understandings of identity was a practice of necessity—one from which we can learn. But in order to do so, we must listen to both carefully, as we live in a time of defenses erected against "others."

At a time when the president of the United States can proudly announce that he is a "nationalist" and the recently elected President of Brazil said that he would rather his son die than be gay, the self-determination of one's identity has become a matter of life and death, whether it is as blunt and final as a death sentence or as slow as the lifelong agony of living a closeted existence.

Later, in the same essay, the authors point out that Cabrera asserted that "there is no way to understand Cuba without studying its Black culture," while Glissant believed "there was always something unknowable, something opaque, inside each person, which, rather than being what divides us, is what links us." As more and more societies demand conformity and enforce an oppressive view of transparency, Glissant's "opacity" presents an alternative.

Cabrera and Glissant did not have time to be cynical or ironic. For them, resistance was vital and could be enacted on many different levels and in many different ways, including in their own writing, which challenges distinctions. Glissant was a poet, philosopher, and novelist. Cabrera was a poet, artist, feminist, and prolific scholar of Afro-Cuban religions. If you are at all interested in any of these issues and the intellectual history of the Caribbean, especially in Cuba and Martinique, the exhibition *Lydia Cabrera and Édouard Glissant: Trembling Thinking* grapples with these issues as well as the complex, intellectual history of the Caribbean.

The exhibition contains *Flamariouss* (2006), a book collaboration between the Korean artist Koo Jeong A and Glissant, *Hommage a Édouard Glissant* (2014), an accordion book of colored brushstrokes by Etal Adnan; and a set of twelve small works done in acrylic and sumi ink on rice paper by Jack Whitten for his painting *Atopolis: For Édouard Glissant* (2014). Three artists of different cultures and races, all of them directly inspired by Glissant.

In Kader Attia's video *Héroes heridos* (2018), a series of interviews with refugees and émigré activists living in Spain, one of the interviewees uses the term "feminization of poverty" to describe the pressure on refugee women to work as prostitutes. As Glissant points out in the film interview, which greets the viewer in the front gallery, capitalism has survived the longest of all systems because it could adapt to world chaos. However, he also believes that all systematized approaches to daily life are ultimately doomed to fail.

While Lam's relationship to Césaire is well known, at least in poetry circles in the United States, his relationship to Cabrera is much less so. And yet they lived near each other in Cuba during World War II, and he did at least one portrait of her, *Retrato de Lydia Cabrera* (*Portrait of Lydia Cabrera*) (1940s). I think it is worth considering that he painted this portrait while his work was undergoing change, and he had begun to recover aspects of his childhood, which included the memory of his godmother, Mantønica Wilson, practicing Santeria, a pantheistic Afro-Cuban religion that was a syncretic combination of Yoruba belief and Catholicism. I see this as an example of Glissant's "creolization," which runs counter to America's narrow definitions of ethnic identity.

Cabrera published over one hundred books during her lifetime, few of which are available in English. *Afro-Cuban Tales*, translated by Alberto Hernandez-Chiroldes and Lauren Yoder is well worth buying. Cabrera was a brilliant, complex figure whose work should be better known to an international audience.[1]

I like that the curators focused on two individuals rather than one. Cabrera and Glissant agreed on many things, but they also went their own ways. One was from Cuba and wrote in Spanish, while the other was from Martinique and wrote in French. This diversity, which is central to the exhibition, is reflected in the array of material the curators presented. There are names that will likely be new to the visitor, including Amelia Peláez, who traveled to France with Cabrera in 1927 to study painting. Her *Mujer con pez* (*Woman with Fish*) (1948) is a knockout. Another highlight is

Tania Bruguera's figurative sculpture *Displacement* (1998/2005), which is made from Cuban earth, glue, wood, nails, and textile. A video projected onto the wall documents the sculpture as a costume being worn at a public street performance in Cuba.

The diversity of materials and approaches is central to the curators' thinking. In this modestly sized exhibition, they introduce us to the multilayered, complex cultures, traditions, and legacies that are part of the history of the Caribbean, amalgams that underscore the significance of interracial and cultural marriages and the possibilities they beget.

The Death of Downtown New York

ONCE UPON A time, the art world—at least as it existed in downtown New York in the 1950s—was incommensurable in myriad ways. I mean, when is the last time you went to a big group show and came across more than half-a-dozen Asian and Asian American artists: Yayoi Kusama, Leo Valledor, Yoko Ono, Nanae Momiyama, Robert Kobayashi, Walasse Ting, and Tadaaki Kuwayama? How many Asian American artists were included in *The Forever Now: Contemporary Painting in an Atemporal World*, which was at the Museum of Modern Art in New York? What happened between the mid-1960s and the present, a little more than a half century? Did Asians stop painting and go into computer programming because that's where the action was? Hollywood erases Asians faster than you can say "anime," and so does the art world, it seems. What forces caused them to become invisible in the mid-1960s, when the art world briefly and begrudgingly acknowledged a handful of Black artists, but seemed to think that America's population was either Black or white?

These are just some of the questions spurred by the exhibition *Inventing Downtown: Artist-Run Galleries in New York City, 1952–1965* at the Grey Art Gallery, New York University, which was curated by Melissa Rachleff, who has done an amazing and thorough job. Rachleff deserves our thanks for amassing a wide and wild range of material, from artwork to documentary photographs to gallery ephemera. She has managed to allot discrete areas to a variety of artist-run galleries and groups in what is a difficult space to organize. Rachleff seems to have left no stone unturned. Driven by curiosity, this is curatorial practice at its best.

For anyone who has come across the name Jean Follett, you can see two wall pieces by her in this exhibition, one of which is in a little-known collection in Athens, Greece. Follett, who studied with Hans Hoffman, began applying layers of paint to found objects placed in a shallow box, to which she added more objects. They are shadow boxes but they are not. They don't look like anything else. They are hybrid works, but that term does not touch upon the strangeness of Follett's art.

Follett was included in three shows at the Museum of Modern Art between 1959 and 1963, including *The Art of Assemblage* (October 4–November 12, 1961), organized by William C. Seitz. That catalog was the first place I saw her work, along with a number of other artists', including Bruce Conner, Jess, and Robert Mallary, alongside Lee Bontecou, Joseph Cornell, Marcel Duchamp, Jasper Johns, Marisol, and Robert Rauschenberg. That kind of openness to different aesthetic positions does not happen anymore.

I don't know what happened to Follett, but I have long been curious about her work, and was more than happy to see it.

Forty years ago, Thomas B. Hess mentioned her in passing in a review of the painter David Budd that appeared in *New York Magazine* (March 7, 1977). Here is the kicker line from that review:

> Some lost their way. Where are Jean Follett and Felix Pasilis? A few died before their time (Gabe Kohn, Sam Goodman, Gandy Brodie). Most have persevered, however, in lives of not quite quiet desperation. They teach a bit, exhibit now and then, while slowly piecing together the historical puzzle that was scattered so brusquely about fifteen years ago, when it seemed, as if on a Monday, they were respected members of a cultural milieu and then, the next Friday, practically the whole art Establishment crossed the street to avoid having to say hello.

Hess writes that this sweeping change took place around 1962. All the artists he mentions have work in the NYU exhibition. I would venture that most are hardly known and the probability is high that none of them have something currently on display in a New York museum.

If 1962 is the dividing line between one art world and what we seem to have inherited—the moneyed domain of expensive, well-produced, shiny fabrication, not to mention the big, industrial, and tastefully rusted—*Inventing Downtown* will bring you back to the period before the "art Establishment crossed the street" into the welcoming arms of the investor class. It is before the art world became arty, and gatekeepers and art-style influencers became more prominent. Between 1952 and '65, the years covered by the exhibition, every kind of scene seemed to be percolating in a rather small geographic area of Manhattan. The epicenter was East Tenth Street, where a bunch of artist-run galleries opened and Willem de Kooning had a studio. Rachleff smartly organizes the show around artist-run galleries, alternative spaces, and groups. Some were short-lived. *Spiral*, a collective of African American artists who met in Romare Bearden's loft on Canal Street, was active from the summer of 1963 until 1965 and had one exhibition. They were trying to negotiate their relationship to race, civil rights, and aesthetics. It could not have been easy. Rachleff also includes the Green Gallery, whose "program," according to the free brochure accompanying the exhibition, "resulted in the narrowing of aesthetic possibilities and the marginalization of many artists." If she left any gallery or alternative scene out, I am unaware of it.

In addition to Follett, there were many artists whose work I hadn't seen before. There were also many surprises from familiar artists, including a garish, Bonnard-inspired *Portrait of Frank O'Hara* (1953–54) by Wolf Kahn. It looks as if the poet is wearing a pink and orange Halloween mask. A few feet away, on the same wall, is a lovely *Portrait of Jane Freilicher* (1957)—a close friend of O'Hara's—

by Jane Wilson. We know the portraits of O'Hara done by Larry Rivers, Fairfield Porter, and Alice Neel, but this one was new to me.

There are also early works by Jim Dine, Dan Flavin, and Allan Kaprow before they became famous for making signature works. Flavin's piece *Apollinaire wounded (to Ward Jackson)* (1959), is made from a crushed can surrounded by oil paint and pencil on Masonite, mounted on plaster on pine in a shallow box. The title is carefully incised into the paint in the upper left corner, while the red hole at the top of the crushed can refers to the poet's head wound, which he got in World War I.

There are abstract paintings by the Black artists Norman Lewis, Hale Woodruff, and Ed Clark, which tell us that the legacy of the 1960s is one of exclusion. That this exclusion began during the Civil Rights Movement does not speak well of the art world. The other thing that struck me is the wide assortment of work. There is no hierarchy between figurative and abstract paintings, nor are there distinctions about materials or processes.

The thickly painted *Heaven and Earth* (1960) by Alfred Jensen is diagonally opposite the thinly painted *Ada Ada* (1959) by Alex Katz. The former is filled with arcane symbols, while the latter depicts the artist's wife twice, wearing a plain blue dress and matching blue shoes. While Hess never says what led up to the sea change in 1962, one cause seems to have been the advent of hierarchical thinking and the other is the growing importance of the collector class. You also have Donald Judd separating painting from the rectangle in his essay "Specific Objects" (1965) as well as reframing the avant-garde phrase of "make it new" to "you cannot do it again."

While Judd's theories might have influenced the thinking and actions of a lot of people, that does not mean he is right: it means that he has a forceful viewpoint powerfully expressed in unequivocal terms. But you can also find the paintings of John Wesley at the Judd Foundation in Marfa, Texas, and so maybe he was not as much of an ideologue as some people want to believe and take comfort in because looking is easier when you know what to look at.

Then there is Clement Greenberg's snobbish term "Tenth Street Touch," which dismissed a lot of artists, including many who did not use a loaded brush or paint the figure. There is the much-ballyhooed claim that art had to be objective, abstract, pure, and even universal—all of which are questionable standards. I think collectors also had something to do with what happened. Whatever the collectors Robert and Ethel Scull did for the art world, they were self-serving narcissists, as Andy Warhol's portrait *Ethel Scull 36 Times* (1963) demonstrates. And, of course, there's commerce, from rising rents to the escalating prices of what looks good on a big, immaculate wall—the "post-easel" picture. These forces together helped produce the perfect storm. In some sense, the art world turned from a place of community to a place of authority.

By bringing us back to the decade before the "art establishment" decided what were the true, quantifiable markers of progress, *Inventing Downtown* reminds us that what we have now was not always the way it was. There are so many things to see and discover—from photographs of interactive paintings by Yoko Ono to George Sugarman's *Four Forms in Walnut* from 1959 (yes, you can carve wood and not be old-fashioned), to a strange and interesting *Self-Portrait in Fur Jacket* (1959) by Marcia Marcus (what happened to her?), to a group of gritty drawings by Emilio Cruz, Red Grooms, and Bob Thompson. Check out the work of Boris Lurie, who was in a concentration camp (1941–45), and then read about him and Sam Goodman and the NO! art movement in *The Outlaw Bible of American Art* (2015), edited by Alan Kaufman. This exhibition brings back a lot of what has been forgotten, overlooked, and thrown under the bus—no doubt with joy. It might not all be good, but to quote another statement that Judd made in "Specific Objects": A work needs only to be interesting. By that standard, everything you see in this exhibition needed to be included.

Another History to Be Learned

In 1969, during the Civil Rights struggle, three Black artists opened Cinque Gallery, which operated until 2004, to "provide a place where the works of unknown, and neglected artists of talent . . ."—primarily Black artists—"would not only be shown but nurtured and developed" (Excerpts from 1969 Cinque Gallery bylaws). The gallery was named after Joseph Cinqué, who led a successful revolt on the Spanish slave ship *La Amistad*. The founders were Romare Bearden (1911–1988), Ernest Crichlow (1914–2005), and Norman Lewis (1909–1979).

During its thirty-five-year existence, Cinque Gallery showed more than 450 artists of color working in various mediums and styles, from representational to abstract. The list, which includes Wifredo Lam, Elizabeth Catlett-Mora, Richard Hunt, Dawoud Bey, Norma Morgan, Whitfield Lovell, and Camille Billops, is impressive. While the mainstream, white art world either ignored or pigeonholed these artists—which raises painful and disturbing questions that have yet to be addressed—the fact that Cinque sustained itself for more than three decades attests to an indisputable fact: the existence of at least two distinct art communities, which were separated along color lines. It is also testimony to the strength and resilience of Black artists more than a century after the end of the Civil War.

The exhibition *Creating Community: Cinque Gallery Artists* at the Art Students League (2021), curated by Susan Stedman (with assistance from Jewel Ham and program curation by Nanette Carter), suggests but does not emphasize that segregation was largely established and maintained by the commercial art world, with museums and other mainstream institutions often following suit.

One reason the exhibition is at the Art Students League is that Bearden, Crichlow, and Lewis taught and/or lectured at the league and were considered important members of that particular community. In the world of art education, they were respected, while in the domain of commercial art galleries they were marginal figures or outliers at best.

In one vitrine, I noticed a Cinque Gallery announcement card for an exhibition, *A Selection of African American Sculpture*, which ran from October 31 to November 25, 1978. Twelve artists were listed on the card: Melvin Edwards, Richard Hunt, Daniel Johnson, Robert Kelly, Ed Love, Valerie Maynard, Howard McCalebb, Algernon Miller, Elizabeth Catlett-Mora, Chris Shelton, Jack White, Jack Whitten.

I was particularly struck by this announcement for this reason: In 1970, Edwards was the first Black sculptor to have a solo show at the Whitney Museum of American Art. Five years earlier, in 1965, he had his first one-person museum exhibition at the Santa Barbara Art Museum. He sold no work from either show and did not receive any offers for gallery representation. Cinque helped keep Edwards's work public.

Similarly, in 1971, William S. Lieberman organized the retrospective *The Sculpture of Richard Hunt* at the Museum of Modern Art in New York. Hunt was the first Black sculptor to be showcased at the museum since a 1937 show featuring self-taught Black sculptor William Edmondson. In 1957, the legendary curator Dorothy C. Miller—who was the first person to show Ellsworth Kelly, Jay DeFeo, Isamu Noguchi, Lee Bontecou, and Jasper Johns in a museum context—purchased Hunt's sculpture *Arachne* (1956) for MoMA; it was the first and only sculpture of his to enter the collection. Hunt was twenty-one at the time. Instead of following this young artist, as MoMA followed young white artists from the same generation, the museum largely forgot about him.

When *Odyssey: Jack Whitten Sculpture, 1963–2017* opened at the Museum of Fine Arts, Houston, the press release stated:

> Although Whitten (1939–2018) has long been celebrated for his work as an innovative abstract painter, this presentation reveals an extensive and entirely unknown body of his work.

The Cinque announcement suggests that this statement is wrong. More importantly, it underscores the complete division between the mainstream white art world and all the other, largely noncommercial art communities made up of people of color.

While none of what I have written is cited in the catalogue accompanying the exhibition, I think the catalogue's publication is an important event for many reasons, including its reproductions of ephemera and mission statements, such as the gallery's 1977 report:

> The Directors knew that many dealers and museum curators were unwilling to 'gamble' on the artistic maturation of young unknown artists. This was especially true for minority painters and sculptors . . . who could not be expected to fulfill their potential unless they were encouraged in a positive way.

It seems to me that this historical gathering should provoke further research as well as exhibitions. Although almost every artist is represented by a single work (which is also reproduced in the catalogue) we are invited to both look and dig deeper—and it is essential that we do so.

It is important to point out that the cross section of artists who showed at Cinque Gallery worked in different mediums and pursued different themes and subjects, that the work made by Black artists between 1969 and 2004 was as diverse as their mainstream counterparts'.

Some of the artists in this exhibition were also associated with Kenkeleba House, which was opened in 1974 by Joe Overstreet, Corrine Jennings, and Samuel C. Floyd to support African

American culture. I mention this because there were a number of important venues that arose in the 1960s and '70s that both overlapped with and supported each other, as well as artists of color working in New York.

This occurred to me while looking at Mildred Thompson's abstract pastel on paper, *Atmospherics #2* (2003), which was credited "courtesy Kenkeleba House."

Another important aspect of Cinque Gallery is that it was open to Black abstract artists. Thompson (1936–2003) was a metaphysical abstract artist preoccupied with the cosmological during the rise of the Black Arts Movement. She moved to Germany, where she lived throughout the 1960s and '70s. In 2019, she had an eye-opening show at Galerie Lelong & Co.

The proximity of an early moody landscape, *Untitled* (1967) by Richard Mayhew, to a haunting oil painting of a deserted mining site, *Abandoned* (1986) by Hughie Lee-Smith, and a large atmospheric engraving, *Elk Lake Adirondack Mountains, NY* (1993) by Norma Morgan, reminded me that I have never seen a show of Black artists who engage with the landscape.

Morgan's landscape is one of the exhibition's highlights. If this work is at all representative of what she achieved in the realm of printmaking, she deserves to be far better known. Shouldn't someone be giving Morgan a museum exhibition?

Morgan's print also reminded me of the importance of the Black artist and master printmaker Robert Blackburn to the community of Black artists, and beyond. It was in his Printmaking Workshop, which he started in 1947, that a number of the artists in this exhibition made their prints.

Another artist whose work I did not know before this exhibition was Ademola Olugebefola; his mixed-media painting *Sun Ra* (1970) contains a reflective moiré pattern that kept changing. Nearby was an emotionally charged abstraction, *Red, White and Black* (ca. 1960) by Charles Alston.

Everywhere I looked, there was something to see and consider, including a slideshow of works by Black artists that were commissioned by the Metropolitan Transportation Authority. Seen by many who ride New York's subways, these public works by Romare Bearden, Robert Blackburn, Jacob Lawrence, Al Loving, and Faith Ringgold are part of the fabric of many lives, something the mainstream art world is showing a few signs of waking up to.

The One Book You Need to Read Right Now Is About Canadian Colonialism

I WANT TO RECOMMEND *Before I Was a Critic I Was a Human Being* (2019) by writer and curator Amy Fung.

Toward the end of the book, I read this sentence:

> Over the last decade, I learned my maternal great grandfather was Sun Baoqi, a foreign minister and premier in the Republic of China.

Along with this family history, from which Fung feels understandably disconnected, her sense of not feeling either "Canadian" or "wholly Chinese" struck a chord.

This is the first sentence of Part I of the prologue:

> I was last notably called a "chink" in 2011 while living in Scotland, that land and people who still fancied calling Indian restaurants "pakis" and Chinese restaurants "chinkies."

Fung ends the paragraph with: "Born in Hong Kong and raised in Canada, my mind has been a deeply colonized place."

By the time I finished the first paragraph, I knew that I would complete this book in one concentrated reading, rather than adding it to my ever-growing pile of books to be finished later.

Before I Was a Critic I Was a Human Being is a collection of linked personal essays about language, displacement, and ownership—about being both an "outsider" and an "intruder" who is complicit in the ongoing suppression of the Indigenous population in Canada, which has a well-established system and set of laws that lead to people becoming either complicit or oppressed.

In order to advance from enemy to ally, Fung had to counteract that soul-crushing relationship in every way that she could. In relation to Canada's art institutions, this has meant turning down jobs, building relationships with people she is expected to ignore, and yelling at a young man who began reciting the poems of Mao Zedong at a party.

Fung's essays begin with growing up in the British colony of Kowloon, Hong Kong, the youngest of three sisters. Later, her mother, Cho Kei, moved the girls to Edmonton, Alberta, Canada (which was once part of the British Empire), while her father, Hing Him, stayed behind and sent money. Fung examines the ways she was colonized in her different environments as well as scrutinizes the use of language in her daily encounters, from childhood to adulthood.

Attending school in Canada from 1988 to 2008, she received what most would consider a high caliber, democratic education, yet, she states, "Everything I learned I have had to unlearn." Language is at the core of Fung's process of learning and unlearning, of doing and undoing:

> As someone who has never seen myself reflected in the nation-state image of Canada, I have ceased looking, and instead started collecting my own stories.

Fung's stories include family histories. (For example, Cho Kei is the youngest child of the first of her father's five wives. There would be twenty-four children in total, eight of whom were her full siblings.) Out of that history, Fung becomes a writer of "snappy copy" and eventually an art critic, learning:

> [In] the 1950s and 1960s, having nowhere else to go, the American art critic Clement Greenberg began a series

> of visits to northern Saskatchewan, attracting a higher than normal concentration of postwar Modernist painters and sculptors to Emma Lake's summer workshop, as they "discovered" the ideal realization of flatness in form and embodiment in the surrounding landscape," which culminates in "reinforcing the false superiority of a European aesthetic."

Fung has a very different sense of space, having spent her early childhood in "the cramped quarters of Kowloon":

> But here: sitting on a rock in an empty farm field in the middle of Saskatchewan. Here I was aware of the sensation of having zero personal space in which to breathe. Being in its diametrical opposite, I could learn to feel the other.

Instead of seeing the vast plains and open skies as a sign of opportunity and nature's amplitude, Fung is reminded that "applying ill-fitting European parameters onto these freshwater grasslands is to be blind to everything that is there." This includes Canada's genocidal history and continuing policies.

In this chapter, the reader also learns that "Saskatchewan is [. . .] one of the most deeply segregated provinces when it comes to Indigenous and settler rights, from the basic necessities to the court of law."

There are so many moments in this and every chapter that leap out at the reader, as Fung comes to terms with her relationship to the various people, places, and histories where she has been invited to "write a feature on a province-wide art project," jury a show, or be a writer in residence.

The subject Fung keeps returning to—and this is the core of the book—is summed up in this paragraph:

> The multicultural myth of Canada has always been undermined by the government's assimilation of and genocidal policies toward Indigenous Nations. Difference against whiteness has never been easily em-

> braced, not for Indigenous Nations, early POC settlers, or Black migrants. More often than not, difference has been so effortlessly met with state violence turned law turned status quo. Diversity works only for whiteness, for those who are happy to benevolently oversee and control diversity in all its frivolous forms, but who will enforce the power of their laws the moment difference seeks actual power.

The reader of this book will learn about Residential Schools, which forcibly separated Indigenous children from their families and sent them miles away to government-sponsored religious schools in order to assimilate the children of "savages" into Euro-Canadian culture. The last state-sponsored Residential School was not closed until 1996. A private Residential School did not close until the following year.

We also learn about the Truth and Reconciliation Commission (TRC) and the discomfort it caused among Fung's peers: "Most of those who had begun dropping TRC into conversations were dropping it like a new band."

> Created as one of several concrete outcomes from the Indian Residential Schools settlement Agreement, the Truth and Reconciliation Commission was tasked to collect and preserve the stories of survivors. Modelled after South Africa's Truth and Reconciliation Commission, which assembled after apartheid had officially ended in 1994, the model has been used by various nations to document their own human rights violations.

Fung has written an important book about Canadian culture and its arts, and how they are bound up with "an extraction economy built in violation of Indigenous land rights and human rights." Her dream is of a future time where "all of us who have gathered here can acknowledge where we came from and how we collectively came to this point." Moving effortlessly from personal anecdote to unsettling recognition of her own complicity to disturbing insight and political statement, Fung's testimony is essential reading.

IV.

A History Waiting to Be Written

Ed Clark's High-Spirited, Abstract Paintings

DAVID HAMMONS'S THOUGHTFUL curation of the exhibition *Ed Clark: Big Bang*, currently at the Tilton Gallery (2014), helps establish a much-needed context for an important Black artist of the New York School, who, now in his late eighties, continues to make boldly exuberant paintings. By including single works by Clark's friends and supporters—Yayoi Kusama, Joan Mitchell, and Donald Judd—Hammons reminds us that Clark had the respect of astute, tough-minded contemporaries, even as curators and critics have repeatedly neglected to acknowledge his contribution over the years.

Clark's inclusion in the traveling exhibition *Blues for Smoke*, curated by Bennet Simpson, which was at the Whitney Museum of American Art, was certainly a step in the right direction. For, as Corinne Robins pointed out in a review from 1997, even the seemingly inclusive chronicler and art historian Irving Sandler failed to mention "Ed Clark or any other artist of color" in his book *The New York School* (1978). The history that Robins alludes to—which is occult and largely kept alive by artists and poets, rather than art historians—needs to be brought further into the light, particularly in New York. I say this because when I first saw work by Clark at the Detroit Institute of Arts Museum and, after that, a particularly memorable, shaped painting from 1957 at the Art Institute of Chicago, I wondered why I had never heard of him before, and what had happened to him. It was as if Clark had been present and active in the late '50s and then mysteriously, he was gone. This, of course, wasn't the case.

Later, I learned that Nicholas Krushenick included Clark, along with Al Held, George Sugarman, Yayoi Kusama, Ronald Bladen, and himself, in the first 1957 Christmas show at the Brata Gallery. A few small pockets of the art world, it seems, were multicultural long before that word entered the discourse. In a 1972 *ARTnews* article, Lawrence Campbell described Clark's shaped painting in the Brata exhibition as the first of its kind. In retrospect, it seems that with the rise of Minimalism, Pop Art, Painterly Realism, and Color Field painting, and the far-reaching influence of formalist criticism, Clark, whose roots are in Abstract Expressionism, got left out, both at the time and in every retelling of what has come to be known as the "Second Generation." Here, it's worth remembering that Donald Judd gave Clark a show in his loft in 1971.

The larger problem is that decades have gone by with few authorities bothering to call attention to Clark's absence, as if everyone—including dealers, curators, collectors, and critics—had gotten their history right the first time. Self-satisfaction is only one of the art world's Achilles' heels. While very few people in New York from the early 1960s on seemed to be paying much attention, particularly to painting that owes something to Abstract Expressionism, Clark continued making bold, innovative work. More importantly—as I hope to make clear—his work subverts a number of commonplace assumptions about Abstract Expressionism, beginning with the long-held charge that it is elitist. It also enlarges our understanding of what various artists did with this loosely defined approach to painting. Like his friend Joan Mitchell, Clark never succumbed to the pressures of Minimalism and Pop Art to reject the materiality of paint and a human touch, as did another contemporary, Al Held.

Moreover, contrary to those who claimed Abstract Expressionism was a purely American development, Clark has openly acknowledged being influenced by Nicolas de Stael's interlocking slabs of impasto paint, which he applied with a palette knife. However, instead of troweling cement-like, slow-drying oil paint, Clark paints on the floor, using a broom to push acrylic paint whose consistency ranges from a watery medium to a creamy paste, in colors that go from white to primaries and secondaries, often mixed with white. Against the unprimed, often slightly dirty canvas, Clark's thick swathes of white paint evoke crème fraîche floating on vichyssoise. There is something innocent and indecent about their pillowy surfaces.

Utilizing an impure approach, which distinguishes him from his more stylistically narrow peers, Clark is likely to combine staining, splattering, and drawing with a broom in a single work. In *Untitled* (2001) and *Untitled* (2005), he stacked wide swathes of thick, velvety paint that horizontally span the surface. Some of the swathes are made of two colors that have been poured together, with the broom mixing them further, while others are layered, one color on top of another. Although they evoke brushstrokes, we instinctively know that the swathes are too wide to have been made by a brush. By pushing them with a broom, Clark connects the history of menial labor and janitorial services with high art and abstract painting. By using a broom as a brush, Clark's bonding of janitorial services and Abstract Expressionist painting challenges the widely received art historical view that it wasn't until Minimalism (Frank Stella's use of a house painter's brushes) and Pop Art (Andy Warhol's silk screens of movie stars and disasters) that artists mixed labor, commercial tools, the everyday, and art. Clark's paintings are performative, while his lush, hybrid forms are simultaneously sculptural and painterly, buoyant and witty.

By using a broom as a brush—and really this should be considered an innovation—it is clear that Clark possesses a remarkable amount of control and possibility with an ungainly instrument. This is most apparent in *Paris* (2009), in which he stacked a series of distinct gestural forms on an unprimed canvas. The variously colored forms, which seem simultaneously solid and liquid, frozen and moving, manmade and lava-like, evoke an adagio act, stones precariously balanced on each other, an abstract totem and a veiled dancer in constant movement. In *Paris*, it is clear that Clark has absorbed as well as transformed the Surrealism of Max Ernst and Joan Miro into something all his own.

Clark's oeuvre is as distinctive and particular, and, in that regard, comparable to the work of other artists who belong to the so-called "Second Generation"—Joan Mitchell, Sam Francis, and Norman Bluhm, for example. He is certainly due the close attention that Mitchell and Francis have received. Clark is an important figure in the history of postwar abstract art, a history that includes African American practitioners, whose work ranges across time and style—from Norman Lewis and Alma Thomas to Cynthia Hawkins, Sam Gilliam, Howardena Pindell, Odili Donald Odita, and Jack Whitten. It is a rich, complex, and little-known history that requires further research and scholarship, not to mention exhibitions and monographs.

Hammons selected eight large paintings that Clark did between 2001 and 2012. They were all done after the artist turned seventy-five. What an eye-popping revelation and joy to see them hung in three spacious rooms of an Upper East Side townhouse. Their enthusiasm is unrivaled and catching.

Does the Museum of Modern Art Even Know about This Great Photographer?

(on Louis Draper)

IN NOVEMBER 1955, four days after Robert Frank was arrested, questioned, and released in Arkansas under the suspicion of being a Communist spy, he took a photograph, *Trolley—New Orleans* (1955), that was included with eighty-two others in his justly famous book *The Americans,* which—we should remember—was first published in France in 1958. Frank's photograph shows a line of white and Black faces looking out the window of a trolley in segregated America, with the whites in front and the Blacks in the back.

I thought of that photograph while walking back home from a retrospective exhibition of photographs by Louis Draper. Draper was born in 1935, a decade after the Swiss-born Frank, in the former capital of the Confederacy, Richmond, Virginia, during the Great Depression. With segregation firmly in place, he would have been one of the people Frank photographed sitting at the back of the trolley in 1955, which was four years after Tennessee Williams's play, set in New Orleans's French Quarter, was turned into the film *A Streetcar Named Desire* (1951), starring Marlon Brando, Vivien Leigh, Kim Hunter, and Karl Malden. Segregation was simply an unspoken fact of that and so many other Hollywood films. Who wants to think about such things while sitting in a movie theater? I suppose only those who have to.

Frank, who was an outsider and white, showed one aspect of

a social order in which Black Americans were both segregated and second-class citizens. The reason why I thought of Frank's outsider status—and the role it played in his photographs—was that Draper lived for many years in Harlem on 127th Street, where he was a member of the Black community and good friends with his neighbor, the poet Langston Hughes. Draper's photographs of Harlem, Mississippi, and Senegal afford us another view, that of an insider turning his views of the community he inhabited and knew well into art.

I suppose what I am getting at is context, and there are many contexts to consider. When I searched the collection of the Museum of Modern Art online, I wasn't surprised to learn that it contains many Frank photographs, but I was disappointed to learn that there were none by Draper. Isn't it time for MoMA to stop treating artists such as Draper, Ray DeCarava, Wifredo Lam, Norman Lewis, Ruth Asawa, Leo Amino, and Alma Thomas as if they are second-class citizens? Sure, things are changing, but am I supposed to be happy when they toss out a few crumbs?

There are more than seventy-five vintage prints in *Louis Draper* at Steven Kasher (2016), a show that should not be missed. In 1957, while he was taking photographs for his college newspaper, Draper saw the catalogue of the exhibition *The Family of Man*, organized by Edward Steichen for the Museum of Modern Art. A landmark exhibit at the time, *The Family of Man* has since been roundly criticized by such well-intentioned figures as Roland Barthes, Susan Sontag, John Berger, and Christopher Philips for being sentimental and humanist. Whatever its success or failure, its catalogue prompted Draper to move to New York City to become a photographer. Soon after arriving in New York, and perhaps feeling a safe distance from the South, Draper took a photograph, *Congressional Gathering* (1959), which shows a row of bed sheets hanging from a clothesline, seemingly at night. Five years earlier, the United States Supreme Court made its landmark decision in Brown vs. Board of Education to end segregation in public education. Four years earlier, Emmett Till, a fourteen-year-old boy, was lynched and brutally—and, I would add, gleefully—murdered in Mississippi, where the perpetrators were later acquitted. Frank's photograph of the New Orleans trolley says a lot about the state of America in the 1950s, but so does Draper's.

Draper's photograph still disturbs, and it should send a shock of recognition through anyone who cares to look. Its title speaks volumes. Despite the Supreme Court's 1954 ruling in Brown vs. Board of Education of Topeka, which declared segregation in public schools "inherently unequal," Draper knew that he lived in a segregated country where members of Congress belonged to the Ku Klux Klan. The sheets, which he photographed in the dark, sag so loosely off the line that the light hitting their top corners evokes the Klan's conical masks. It connects domestic cleanliness with racial cleansing. Draper's image summons the deep fear that must have been felt by every Black person in America; this was what it meant to exist in a one-sided, lawless society. Till's murder and the acquittal of his killers confirmed it. As much as I love Frank's photograph, Draper's speaks to another, deeper part of us—the one where the fear of faceless authority churns. As recent events again make clear, no matter how minor the supposed crime, some people don't get out of jail alive.

In 1963—in the midst of the Civil Rights Movement—Draper was one of the founding members of Kamoinge Workshop, a group of fifteen Black photographers. As the introduction to their first portfolio of work stated, this group's "creative objectives reflect a concern for truth about the world, about society, about themselves." Ray DeCarava was the Kamoinge Workshop's first director. Hughes, who was friends with Henri Cartier-Bresson, introduced him to Draper, who got him to speak to the members of Kamoinge. This way of transmitting knowledge is basic to any art or literary group, and it isn't about networking or social climbing.

Timeless: Photographs by Kamoinge (2015), edited by Anthony Barboza and Herb Robinson, coedited by Vincent Alabiso, with a foreword by Quincy Troupe, is a beautifully produced book documenting this group's activities. Although not acknowledged on the cover, Deborah Willis has contributed an essay to it. This book is an essential document to the history of American photography. In celebration of its publication, commemorating the group's fiftieth anniversary, there was an exhibition, *Kamoinge: Timeless,* at the Wilmer Jennings Gallery at Kenkeleba House on the Lower East Side.

There are photographs by Draper of Black children playing on the streets, crossing the street as they walk home from school, big smiles on their faces. This is a world that he was part of, and knew well. If you think of them as social documents, you will miss the art. There is a portrait, *Malcolm X, 369th Armory, Harlem* (1964), in which only a sliver of Malcolm's face is visible, the rest immersed in shadow, thinking. Draper is using the available light and seems to make himself invisible—he wants to see rather than be seen.

Sometimes the children Draper portrays look defiant, and why wouldn't they be? In *Boy and H, Harlem* (1961), a skinny teenage boy, playing stickball, stands beside a wall. What does the "H" crudely painted on the wall behind him stand for? What associations does it stir up? What about the word "night" hand-lettered on a store window in *Young Man Smoking, New York* (ca. 1965) that is cropped by the photograph's right edge so that we read "nig"? On the other side of the cropped sign, a boy in a hat, looking all grown up, stares at the camera, smoking. In this and other portraits, the available light caresses the faces, and a moment of tenderness filters throughout.

In *Boy and Movie Poster, Harlem, New York City* (1968), a young boy is running down the street. Above him, and spanning the length of the photograph, is a poster of famous Hollywood stars, all white. The juxtaposition is all, just ask the person in the photograph. In *Untitled (Snowy footprints on sidewalk)* (ca. 1965), who is walking in the snow, hidden under an umbrella, might remind you how difficult it is for some to make their way in an all-white world.

Ming Smith's Necessary Angels

MING SMITH WAS the first woman—and for a long time the only one—to join the Kamoinge Workshop, a group of fifteen Black photographers founded in 1963, in the midst of the Civil Rights Movement and the beginning of a convulsive period in American history. One impetus for the group was self-determination: the fifteen members wanted to document Black life, as well as push back against the limited racial views that had been propagated by white photographers. The first director was Roy DeCarava, who characterized the photographs taken by members as "creative objectives [which] reflect a concern for truth about the world, about society, about themselves." The strongest members of the group turned documentary photography into art. While Smith took black-and-white photographs of her changing milieu—New York neighborhoods, including Harlem; jazz musicians; her trips to Europe and Africa—her work is closer to dreams and memories than to *The Decisive Moment* (1952) of Henri Cartier-Bresson. At first glance, Smith's photographs do seem to capture moments like the ones Cartier-Bresson described in his influential concept, where a narrative moment comes together in a single image (and Smith once made a portrait of Cartier-Bressson). However, if we look longer, we see that in her hands the documentary becomes about time slipping past and history haunting the present, rather than about the frozen moment and timelessness.

Previously, I have written about two members of the Kamoinge Workshop, Louis Draper and Anthony Barboza. There is a wonderful book, *Timeless: Photographs by Kamoinge* (2015), edited by Anthony Barboza and Herb Robinson, coedited by Vincent Alabiso, with a foreword by Quincy Troupe, which I have called "an essential document to the history of American photography." Smith is both a part of this history—which still needs to be addressed—and a singular figure.

The gallery press release for the exhibition *Ming Smith* at Steven Kasher Gallery (2017) bills it as "the first major retrospective of the photographer's work." There are more than seventy-five vintage black-and-white prints in the exhibition. A smaller retrospective survey of thirty-three photographs, *Ming Smith Photographs: 1977–2010*, was held at the June Kelly Gallery in 2010. Aside from their size, the big difference between the two exhibitions is that the current one focuses on her black-and-white photographs and does not include any of her hand-painted photographs. In her use of blurred images, and the push from the documentary to abstraction through an emphasis on light and shadow, Smith comes across as one who knows the rules but refuses to play by them. This might require some viewers to adjust to Smith's vision of the world, which is not like that of other street photographers who began working in black-and-white photography during the 1970s, but it is definitely worth it.

There are so many memorable works in this show, I wish a comprehensive monograph existed on Smith's work—say two hundred images to show the diversity of what she has achieved. It is certainly time: if the history of what Americans know about themselves and art is going to change—and it damn well better—Smith's work is part of that process.

In *Dakar Roadside with Figures, Dakar, Senegal* (1972), a woman is walking down the street—from right to left—into a strong wind, and a white cape-like fabric, which is attached to the hem of her white dress and shoulders, billows out behind her like a sail. A gray wall forming her backdrop spans the length of the photograph, tilting from the photograph's left edge to its right. The swollen bend of the tree trunk in front of the woman extends to the left, mirroring the swell of the cape, which is arcing to the right, while the leafy crown of the tree reaches over the woman's head.

On the photograph's far right, two men are under a similar tree, which is perfectly vertical: it is as if there are two weather zones, with the wind between the trees and calmer climes on the rightmost edge. The angle of the wall, the echo of the woman and the tree, and the sense that there are two different weather patterns are just part of what makes this photograph—its decisive moment—so enchanting. Everything is in tension with everything else; an active moment has been preserved, and the woman has been imbued with sculptural presence. She is a distinct part of this world, and she is in some sense separate from it, the lone citizen of her domain.

In another photograph, *Sun Ra Space II, New York* (1978, printed ca. 2000), Ra's glittering headgear and scintillating scarf fluttering into the air look like something otherworldly and cosmic. Members of Ra's band are behind him, playing as they follow their leader. Instead of focusing on Ra, Smith has keyed the photograph to the light as it struck the scarf, which is perfectly situated to become the center of attention. It's as if Ra has transcended his corporeal presence.

A number of writers have already said smart things about Smith, and I am happy to call attention to them. This is what Holland Cotter wrote in his review of Smith's show at June Kelly, which included a photograph in which the face of James Baldwin hovers in the clouds over Harlem.

> It's hard to think of another photographer who could set a misty head shot of the writer James Baldwin in a bank of dark clouds over the Harlem skyline and get away with it, but she does, and more than that she creates something heartfelt and gorgeous in its deep feeling and high sophistication.

In this series of photographs, Smith honors those who contributed their vision to a community that has largely existed on a separate track from what is commonly called mainstream society. They are seen as guardian spirits.

A sense of community, and of individuals who are often isolated within it, is one of Smith's enduring themes. In the photograph *American Dream, Harlem, New York* (ca. 1972), which is of a large dirty cutout of Santa Claus lying on its side, hoisting a bottle of soda, Smith stirs up a complex of feelings: this is not the white-bearded jolly fatso bringing good cheer. In another photo, *Kites Inside, Columbus, Ohio* (ca. 1972), two kites are suspended from the ceiling of an apartment, near a bare bulb. One kite has a round face with its tongue sticking out, while the other is more of a silhouette, and resembles a turkey falling from the sky. The image is comic and disturbing. Is the bare bulb the closest that the kites get to the sun?

In another recent review, Maurice Berger wrote:

> Ms. Smith's subjects are often suspended between visibility and invisibility: faces turned away, or are blurred or shrouded in shadow, mist or darkness, a potent metaphor of the struggle for African-American visibility in a culture in which Black men and women were disparaged, erased or ignored.[1]

The rich and varied evocation of passing moments, memories, and dreams that we encounter in Smith's photographs are things that the art world has spent decades ignoring. We cannot let it continue.

Teju Cole Has Not Stopped Looking or Thinking

TEJU COLE WAS born in Kalamazoo, Michigan, in 1975, raised in Lagos, Nigeria, and educated in England and America, where he earned a degree in art history. The author of three well-received books (two fiction and one collection of essays), he is the photography critic for the *New York Times Magazine*. By any measure, he is a major figure in American arts and letters. However, in a world where critics and commentators are known to post selfies and become celebrities, Cole does something very different, and it shows in his work: he keeps a low profile and remains humble.

More importantly, Cole has never disconnected himself from the anonymous figures living on the margins of our wasteful, consumer-happy society, nor has he exploited them. He doesn't turn them into heroes in his fiction, and they are not the center of attention in his photographs; in other words, he doesn't attempt to grant them a status they do not achieve in real life. Although the humanitarian thrust of his work is consistent, he does one thing in his fiction and essays, and another in his photographs, which are being exhibited in his first solo show, *Teju Cole: Blind Spot and Black Paper* at Steven Kasher Gallery (2017).

The exhibition is in celebration of his fourth book, *Blind Spot*, published in 2017 by Random House with a foreword by Siri Hustvedt. *Blind Spot* contains more than 150 color photographs, each paired with text by Cole. Together, they form a travel diary, as the photographs were taken in different cities and places throughout the world: Mexico City, Wannsee, Qadisha Valley, Lagos, Beirut, Nairobi, Old Goa, Seoul, Ubud (Indonesia), and Auckland. According to Hustvedt, the book's title is personal:

> One morning in 2011, Teju Cole woke up blind in one eye. He suffered from papillophlebitis, perforations to his retina. The disappearance of sight in one eye makes depth perception impossible, and Cole informs the reader he had trouble walking.

Later, quoting Cole, Hustvedt writes: "The photography changed after that. The looking changed."

As a novelist, Cole has been described as a postcolonial flâneur who is receptive to (and is able to channel) the stories of the disenfranchised. He gives the Other a place to speak in his or her words. Here it might be useful to recall how the great French poet and art critic Charles Baudelaire, who originated the term, described the flâneur:

> The crowd is his element, as the air is that of birds and water of fishes. His passion and his profession are to become one flesh with the crowd. For the perfect flâneur, for the passionate spectator, it is an immense joy to set up house in the heart of the multitude, amid the ebb and flow of movement, in the midst of the fugitive and the infinite. To be away from home and yet to feel oneself everywhere at home; to see the world, to be at the center of the world, and yet to remain hidden from the world—impartial natures which the tongue can but clumsily define.

Cole recognizes that in the postmodern world, the possibilities for the flâneur have changed radically: can he or she still become one flesh with the crowd or even with another individual?

This is what I meant when I wrote earlier in this essay that Cole keeps a low profile and remains humble. As a photographer, you feel that he recognizes invisibility and does not give you permission to be invasive. Most of the photographs in the exhibition have no people in them. For those that do, except for one photograph of a boy taken in Brazzaville, which we see two versions of, nearly everyone we do see has his or her back to the camera.

These photographs, most of which were taken in New York City, echo a well-known viewpoint taken by many photographers, from Rudy Burckhardt and Lee Friedlander to Vivian Maier. The question (or challenge) for Cole, who no doubt knows all of their work, was this: what can I bring to this view, given my awareness of who and what has preceded me?

In one photograph, titled *New York City, May 2015* (2015)—all his work is titled by the city where the photograph was taken—we see a man in a gray sweatshirt, its hood over his head, standing at a payphone. The text, which is included in the framed photograph, reads as follows:

> What is he saying? To whom is he talking? He is secret in public. The hood is extra secrecy, like the veil Timanthes put over Agamemnon. The phone box frames him in a way that makes me think of a prisoner whose singular lifeline is the telephone that reaches the outside world. Moments later I will encounter the blond woman in green. But I don't know that yet. She's still in the future. Who in these days still uses a pay phone? There are still pay phones? Is he calling someone collect? (Again, I think of imprisonment.) The one to whom he speaks cannot see him: speech without a face. Why do I feel like I have seen him before? [Chris] Marker says remembering is not the opposite of forgetting but rather its lining. Imagine, for a moment, that every face you cannot see is your own face, but years later. The future is lined with your future face.

Cole's pairing of photograph and text creates a third thing. By asking whether pay phones exist or not, he locates the photograph in time, recognizes his boundedness. The questions he asks in his text—which functions as a kind of voiceover, as in Marker's great film *La Jetée* (1962), composed almost entirely of still shots—become a point of entry for the viewer.

The texts and photographs open up avenues for each other that change from work to work, from the attitude of an impartial observer to that of a historically aware global citizen. In *Baalbek, May 2016* (2016), Cole pairs a photograph of a man standing on a tree branch, attending to the tree, with a text about vertigo and jet lag, and highlights the shift from spatial displacement to chronological displacement: "Finally we had figured out how to move across time faster than time moves across us."

Cole's filmic pairing of photograph and text turn the images into shots from an ongoing chronicle of what he has seen and the states of consciousness it has provoked in him, the unexpected connections and associations. These include biblical texts, classical texts, yesterday's and today's news, memories, research, and much else. They are a record of a man's attempt to stay alive and alert, open to the world he is literally passing through. Imagine a diary in which the author is not the center of attention. This is what Cole does in the age of selfies, and I find that achievement remarkable and moving.

Imagine a photograph in which an anonymous migrant speaks, as in *Beirut, May 2016* (2016): a precipitous view of granite blocks rises above the ocean. One of the blocks, which has writing on its top, resembles a coffin. Cole's commentary reads:

> My darling. They said we wouldn't cross tonight. Now they say we must. My phone is dying. There is a pregnant woman here and she won't stop crying. I will send you a Facebook message tomorrow, inshallah.

Recently, Cole wrote a *New York Times Magazine* review of four photographers—three outsiders and one insider—whose shared subject are the people of Indigenous communities, particularly in the Americas. He ended the review, titled, "Getting Others Right" (June 13, 2017), with this observation:

> Photography is particularly treacherous when it comes to righting wrongs, because it is so good at recording appearances. Capturing how things look fools us into thinking that we've captured their truth. But appearance is bare fact. Combined with intuition, scrupulous context and moral intelligence, it has a chance to become truth. Unalloyed, it is worse than nothing.

I think anyone who reads these lines would be curious to see Cole's photographs, especially after recognizing that his test of a photograph is how thoroughly it combines "intuition, scrupulous context and moral intelligence." This goes beyond setting the bar high. It challenges the photographer to do more than take pictures. (Here the word "take" is something to consider. If you can take a photograph, can you do the opposite?)

I don't think it is a stretch to say that "moral intelligence" is in short supply these days, especially when it comes to our elected and appointed officials, some of whom believe that the earth is around five thousand five hundred years old, that climate change is a Chinese plot, that lying about one's accomplishments is acceptable, and that Black people should be further isolated from power through gerrymandering. It is in this world that Cole has found a way to give us states of consciousness—of works that look outward and inward—that challenge us to ask: what must I do to keep looking and thinking in a world that offers distractions of every kind?

V.

Looking at America

The Art of Luis Jiménez

AT FIRST GLANCE, Luis Jiménez's voluptuous, fiberglass public sculptures and large, full-bodied drawings seem to be about a mythic America populated by larger-than-life figures. And yet, even as we recognize some of the figures in his art, we begin sensing that the seeming simplicity of his work is deceptive, and that there is a much more complex and powerful impulse that is being articulated, celebrated, and explored. For one thing, Jiménez consciously commemorates individuals and ethnicities that are not ordinarily elevated or even recognized. A populist artist, who possesses a gently satirical eye when it comes to dealing with certain familiar types, Jiménez's subjects have included caballeros, steelworkers, sodbusters, honky tonk habitués, illegal immigrants crossing the border, and lowriders—many of whom are part of the invisible mass of Hispanic Americans upon which large parts of America and its material success have been built. And although Jiménez *is* a populist artist, he is not naive about his subject matter. Rather than dressing up familiar tales in new clothes, he has strived to reconstruct both this country's unfamiliar tales and those that are disregarded, forgotten, or misrepresented—from the Aztec warrior Cuauhtémoc, whom the Spanish conquistadors burned to death, to a Native American warrior alone on his horse in the sunset.

Since the mid-1960s, when Jiménez began working in fiberglass, choosing to define an aesthetic and cultural space outside the mainstream art world and its preoccupation with Pop Art, Minimalism, and linear views of art history's progress, he has dedicated himself to making a wide range of marginalized individuals as well as ethnic and social groups appear center stage. One of the underlying reasons his public sculptures have been controversial is that he keeps bringing into view that which has been overlooked, reminding us that America's history is made up of many tales stemming from different cultures and ethnicities. At the same time, he does not see himself as a spokesman for those who are silenced or forgotten, and he is not in this regard a political artist. If anything, he has found a way to enable these individuals and groups to tell their stories through the sculptures and drawings he makes. It is a telling that is modest and direct, while swelling with dignity and pride.

Luis Jiménez simultaneously bridges and imaginatively restates three seemingly divergent currents in twentieth-century art: the American regionalist movement of the 1930s, particularly as it culminated in the work of Thomas Hart Benton; the paintings and public murals of Mexican artists, such as Diego Rivera, José Clemente Orozco, and David Alfaro Siqueiros; and the attention paid to ordinary and familiar things by Pop artists, particularly Claes Oldenburg and James Rosenquist. Jiménez is not nostalgic for these movements and does not fully subscribe to the mythic pageantry of Benton, the fiery rhetoric of the Mexican muralists, or to Oldenburg's slyly ironic stance about things. His vision is darker and grittier than Benton's, gentler and more lyrical than Siqueiros's, and more robust and directly engaging than Oldenburg's.

At the same time, what Jiménez recognizes about these twentieth-century movements is that the artists belonging to them were, in the case of Benton, Rivera, and Oldenburg, civic-minded individuals. Jiménez is also civic-minded, but, unlike Benton, he is not against the latest developments in modern art. Known for his use of modern, non-art materials—spray paint and fiberglass—Jiménez is very much a contemporary artist whose roots are in Pop Art, as much as they are in the modernism of the Mexican muralists, the regionalism of Benton and Grant Wood, and the stories and popular myths he learned growing up in the Mexican American community in El Paso. Like Oldenburg, Jiménez focuses on what we overlook or take for granted. The difference is that Jiménez is concerned with individuals and groups that mainstream society overlook or are prejudiced against, while Oldenburg concentrates on mundane things that we use or see in our everyday life—the eraser or toilet. By picking these commonplace objects, Oldenburg is implicitly proposing that America is homogeneous, more alike than different—an attitude shared by Andy Warhol. However, by focusing on different, even contentious subcultures within the ethnic community of Mexican Americans, Jiménez recognizes America's heterogeneity, and that it is more different than alike.

A Mexican American who was born in El Paso, Texas, in 1940, Jiménez's maternal grandfather was a glassblower and his paternal grandfather a carpenter. His father worked in, and eventually owned, a sign-painting shop that became known throughout the Southwest for its neon signs. By the time Jiménez was in his midteens, he had worked in his father's shop and mastered the techniques of welding and spray-painting.

Jiménez's pride in his father was evident when, in the summer of 1988, he drove me around El Paso, pointing to his father's signs that remained in use, including one that was a sculpture of a polar bear commissioned by the owner of Crystal Cleaners. Luis stopped the car and told me the story of how and when his father set out to make a polar bear in his shop, having never actually seen one.

Jiménez's background consists of being raised in two traditions: a family that valued craftsmanship, and the Latinx community that lives and works in a border town on the edge of the larger community known as America. El Paso is an entry point for immigrants, and can be seen as a landlocked version of San

Francisco or New York. It is a city where the descendants of early settlers and the newly arrived live side by side, a place where old and new tales flourish and mutate. It is these and other narratives that Jiménez has made a part of his ongoing project, which is the redefinition of the uses of public sculpture, the restating of popular American myths, and the recovery of unknown or forgotten stories. On the simplest level, Jiménez's project can be said to be the skillful integration of three separate perceptual modes: the use of lowbrow materials (spray paint and fiberglass); a reexamination of the context and purpose of public sculpture; and the making (writing) and remaking (rewriting) of the untold tales and popular myths about the formation of the continually changing American West.

Often the most popular myths are a way of tidying up the past, making it into a story that is emblematic of the larger culture's narrow and biased self-interests. Jiménez does not try to make the past into a neat picture, something whose surface belies the depths of what actually occurred. Andy Warhol, for example, made a portfolio of prints entitled *Cowboys and Indians* (1986), which included images of John Wayne, Annie Oakley, George Armstrong Custer, Teddy Roosevelt, and Geronimo. In Warhol's eyes, all the images and their meanings were equal and to some degree interchangeable. However, to include Wayne, Custer, the Indian Head nickel, and Geronimo in the same portfolio, as if they are typical "cowboys and Indians," is to turn everything into an image, which, according to Museum of Modern Art curator Riva Castleman, "portrayed nothing less than the universal view of America's once enchanted and powerful past." Embraced by MoMA and the New York art world, Warhol's saccharine vision of America's past is closer to Disneyland and Hollywood's views than to the actual individuals and events that shaped the American West.

Jiménez does something very different from Warhol. In *End of the Trail (with Electric Sunset)* (1971), he represents a Native American on his horse buoyed up by the glow of the setting sun. The unlikely combination of this symbolic image with modern industrial materials (fiberglass, brightly colored spray paint, and electric bulbs) makes the sculpture immediately bold and yet emotionally distant. Formally, Jiménez underscores the paradox of immediacy and aloofness by making the rider, horse, and sunset into one brightly colored unit that is also a cold body. Meanwhile, the electric bulbs (a sign of technological progress) remind us that Jiménez has made up his sculpture, that it is a fiction rather than an attempt to be realistic.

Whereas Warhol's prints depend upon the viewer's ability to recognize his subjects, which serves to verify their truthfulness, Jiménez's sculpture compels the viewer to actively engage in reading it to adduce all of its possible meanings. The setting sun can be understood as a symbol marking the demise of both an individual and his way of life, but the sun, as we know, also returns. Seen this way, the sculpture evokes the end of something known and the beginning of something not yet known—an optimistic belief in change.

At the same time, the bulbs complicate our reading of *End of the Trail (with Electric Sunset)*. Have they superseded the sun because they can provide light at all hours of the day and night? Are they meant to signify the triumph of technology over a nomadic way of life? Are they meant to turn the sculpture into a sign of some sort, an advertisement? And if so, what is being advertised?

The difference between Warhol and Jiménez is that the former used either bland or celebrity images the viewer is meant to recognize immediately, while the latter reinterprets charged symbols in order to embody a range of meanings that both challenge and undermine the way we understand the world we live in. In *End of the Trail (with Electric Sunset),* Jiménez's use of fiberglass, spray paint, and electric bulbs remind us that the subjugation of Native Americans was one consequence of technological advances: the materials become the sarcophagus encasing the figure. By making him out of painted fiberglass, Jiménez reminds us that the death of Native Americans and their culture is ongoing, that it is not simply a closed chapter in a history book. The sculpture is both a poignant testament to their ongoing death and a sensitive registering that we are all encased in the modern age.

Jiménez began his career as a figurative sculptor working in traditional materials. He studied at the University of Texas in Austin, and then at the Cuidad Universitaria, Mexico City, where he was able to see the murals of Rivera and Siqueiros up close, as well as visit nearby pre-Columbian temples. All of this adds up to a very different set of references that Jiménez can draw upon. In the mid-1960s, he switched from working in wood to making molds for fiberglass and polyester resin sculptures, such as *Little TV Models* (1965-66) and *Black Torso* (1966). In a pencil drawing, *Chicana Face Emerging from Blond TV Image* (1967), Jiménez began defining one direction his work would take. In contrast to the Pop artists, who for the most part failed to acknowledge that America was made up of people who came from different, not necessarily white cultures, Jiménez focuses his attention on the Chicanos, an ethnic group the mass media ignored, stereotyped, and often demonized during the 1960s, and to some degree continues to do so even now. While Pop Art likely played a part in Jiménez's decision to use fiberglass, his own background in his father's shop and growing up Mexican American in El Paso gave him a very different understanding of contemporary culture and craft from the outset.

Made during the height of Pop Art, *Chicana Face Emerging from Blond TV Image* is an early indication of Jiménez's decision to uncover that which mainstream society and the mass media had rendered invisible, covered over, stereotyped, and misrepresented. His subject matter consists of people, the news, and history that America ignores or marginalizes, rather than the famous celebrities and well-known consumer items Warhol chose to incorporate into his art. Jiménez's notion of popular culture goes against the idea that everyone in America shares the same second-hand experience, that all our lives are fundamentally the same. His work recognizes that for all the overarching narratives that are used to present America as "enchanted," there are regional, ethnic alternatives that are equally as beguiling, maybe more so.

Rafael Ferrer's Gift of Two Dried-Up Pineapples

THERE WERE MORE than thirty works in the exhibition *Rafael Ferrer: Calor* at the Adam Baumgold Gallery (2013). While most were works on paper, one work, *Lam* (1996), was a protruding wall piece made of three painted and incised gourds joined together by metal rods. This is not the first time that Ferrer has alluded to or named the great Cuban modernist Wifredo Lam (1902–1982) in his work and, I suspect, it won't be the last.

In 1954, Ferrer, who was born in Puerto Rico in 1933, traveled to Europe and met Lam, who, recognizing a kinship, dedicated and gave one of his drawings to him. Lam, whose father was Chinese and whose mother was Afro-Cuban, understood the effects of colonialism. At the outbreak of World War II, Lam left Europe, where he had been for nearly two decades, and sailed back to Cuba. During his voyage back, Lam was briefly imprisoned in Martinique, where he met the Martinican poet Aimé Césaire (1913–2008), who helped found the Négritude movement in French literature and was a teacher of Frantz Fanon (1925–1961), author of *Black Skin, White Masks* (1952) and *The Wretched of the Earth* (1961). In 1943, while in Cuba, Lam did his great painting *The Jungle,* which the Museum of Modern Art, New York, hung for years by the coatroom and, more recently, in the second-floor hallway by the men's room.

I mention this nexus of connections because Lam's influence

on Ferrer was both artistic and cultural. By making a sculpture out of gourds and evoking the older artist in the guise of a musician, Ferrer, who is a renowned Afro-Cuban drummer, links himself to Lam, who once stated:

> I decided that my painting would never be the equivalent of that pseudo-Cuban music for nightclubs. I refused to paint cha-cha-cha. I wanted with all my heart to paint the drama of my country, but by thoroughly expressing the Black spirit, the beauty of the plastic art of the Blacks. In this way I could act as a Trojan horse that would spew forth hallucinating figures with the power to surprise, to disturb the dreams of the exploiters. I knew I was running the risk of not being understood either by the man in the street or by the others. But a true picture has the power to set the imagination to work, even if it takes time.

Ferrer has had at least two distinct careers. Between the late 1960s and early '70s, he used such ephemeral materials as ice, leaves, and cyclone fencing to make temporary installations whose existence is largely recorded in photographs and drawings. He once filled a gallery elevator with leaves from floor to ceiling. During this period, he was associated with artists such as Allan Kaprow, Gordon Matta-Clark, Alan Saret, and others who were trying to work outside the white box.

At the same time, as the dates of his exhibition *RAFAEL FERRER, Works on Paper, A Survey, 1952–2012* at the Lancaster Museum of Art indicate, drawing played an important role, as it has throughout his practice. In his second career, which began in 1972, shortly after he had a show of his temporary installations at the Museum of Contemporary Art, Chicago, Ferrer seemed to do an abrupt about-face. Inspired by the artists associated with the Hairy Who and the Chicago Imagists (Jim Nutt, Roger Brown, Art Green, Ed Flood, and others), Ferrer got back in touch with his Surrealist roots. He also became an artist of place. This is most evident in his drawings on navigational maps in oil stick and other media, which he began doing in the '70s.

A number of these are in the show at Adam Baumgold. In the large map drawing *La Luna y La Palma II* (1979), Ferrer uses the map's grid to define squares of different colors, thus linking a commonplace modernist device with mapping and colonialism. The image of the quarter moon and palm remind us that a map is a static abstraction, which is superseded by the actual place and the passage of time.

In another, smaller map drawing, *51 State Bridge* (2005), Ferrer grids off a map and fills it with a mixture of the real and the fanciful, while recalling pre-Columbian navigational charts. Along the bottom of the map, in a gridded area of gray-and-white parallelograms, he has written in cursive letters the Spanish word *pesadilla* (nightmare). Above *pesadilla,* Ferrer has stacked two words, *migraña* (migraine) and *memoria* (memory). Elsewhere, he has labeled Cuba the "Real South Beach" and connected it to Florida with the "51st State Bridge."

Another area is marked "Valet Parking" and "Free Disney Ruins." Satire is a way of turning anger and critique into humor, and Ferrer has more than enough of it to go around. In the margin between the map and the paper's bottom edge, Ferrer has written "SUR REAL." He has written "SOUTH" in the margin along the map's top edge, a clear sign of how upside-down the world has become.

Christopher Columbus brought the pineapple from Guadeloupe back to Europe on his second voyage. Within a short time the pineapple became a symbol for hospitality, and one can still see it carved into marble columns or cast as doorknockers of houses built during the colonial and antebellum periods. It is hard to imagine that Ferrer, who lived for many years in Philadelphia, never saw one used in this way. In the ink drawing *Untitled (Pineapple),* dated 1983 and the oil stick on paper *Dos Pinas Secas (Two Dry Pineapples),* 1990, Ferrer depicts pineapples as isolated or fallen objects.

In *Dos Pinas Secas* the oil stick's rich texture and the dense green of the ground are inviting to the eye, but, at the same time, his use of black and reddish-brown to depict the fruit are signs that the pineapple is a dead thing, incapable of providing nourishment. Surely this is one of the binds Ferrer finds himself in as an artist. He wants to be both critical and nourishing, sharp and sensual. In his ability to negotiate both sides of this conundrum, Ferrer becomes—as Lam did before him—a Trojan horse.

In the oil painting *Dulzura (Sweetness)* (1993), Ferrer depicts a close-up view of a Black woman seen from behind. She is balancing a large bowl of pineapples, bananas, mangoes, and gourds on her head. Her left hand grips a bag whose contents are cropped by the painting's bottom edge. What appears to be a gourd is held in her right hand, and a shopping bag is looped over her forearm. Ahead of her we see a river that she will presumably cross. The roof of a house—her possible destination—is visible on the far shore. Nothing is spelled out. This is the opposite of tourist art, which always shows the natives, so to speak, happily going about their business for the entertainment of the omniscient viewer.

At the same time, and I cannot stress this enough, Ferrer does not want the viewer to see this woman as a victim or even as a symbol for something larger. In fact, in his use of dark and light blues, dark salmon pink, and various greens, browns, and yellows, the painting could be understood as being about different intensities of color. And if Ferrer's restating of the grid and use of color isn't enough to convince us of his imaginative powers, we should consider the mystery and dignity he infuses into his depiction of this woman on her return trip from the market. We see her, but she neither sees us nor acknowledges our presence. She is too busy with living to care about what we think. It is this understanding of autonomy and independence that has guided Ferrer throughout his long and adventurous career.

Meeting Places

(on Siah Armajani)

SIAH ARMAJANI (1939–2020) was interested in meeting places and passageways, walking and sitting, movement and reflection. His work is not confined to being an aesthetic object you contemplate; it can also be something you can use. His vocabulary consists of chairs, tables, lecterns, bridges, stairs, lighting, and literary inscriptions—stuff that is part of our everyday lives. The things he constructs tend to serve multiple purposes, including an actual function and a metaphorical one. In addition to being operational, Armajani believes objects should be ornamental, and, in that regard, capable of enhancing our lives. A rare melding, Armajani's civic-minded, socially conscious aesthetic joins the literal and the figurative, the actual and historical, without becoming didactic.

Nearly 375 feet in length, his *Irene Hixon Whitney Bridge* (1988) in Minneapolis, Minnesota, where he lived and worked for many years, spans seventeen lanes of highways and streets, and physically connects the Minneapolis Sculpture Garden with Loring Park, an inner-city commons that was designed by Frederick Olmstead, who oversaw the building of New York's beloved Central Park and Brooklyn's Prospect Park. The building of the freeways, which helped connect different parts of Minneapolis-St. Paul, ultimately separated the lakefront park from the part of the city surrounding the Walker Art Center. In the early 1980s, when the Minnesota Sculpture Garden was expanded, city planners recognized that a bridge from the Sculpture Garden to Loring Park would connect the two areas of rejuvenation by passing over seventeen lanes of highways and streets set into an area less than four hundred feet wide.

The city commissioned Armajani, a longtime Minneapolis resident, to design the bridge. Within the physical joining, Armajani made other connections, such as bringing together three different architectural structures of bridge (truss, arch, and suspension) into one dynamic, eye-catching, workable structure. Visually distinct, the three kinds of bridge structures played important roles in the history of Minneapolis-St. Paul and the joining together of the major metropolitan areas built around the Mississippi, Minnesota, and St. Croix rivers in east central Minnesota. By incorporating the three structural forms into its overall design, the *Irene Hixon Whitney Bridge* recounts a part of the area's history, as each of the structural designs had been used to traverse one of the area's rivers.

Dreaming up as well as constructing things at vastly different scales, Armajani has made drawings and plans for actual objects and impossible-to-realize projects. In addition to bridges, plazas and other large public spaces, he has made smaller pieces, ranging from enclosed areas large enough for one or two individuals to stand or sit in to small, discrete models that can be held in one's hands. Drawing inspiration from Russian Constructivism, Bauhaus design, American Shaker furniture and architecture, and vernacular architecture, Armajani has made works that are simultaneously serious and quixotic, direct and allusive.

Built as a temporary structure in 1970, *Bridge Over Tree* gracefully steps over a lone tree growing in a field. After ascending and descending over the tree and travelling a short distance, the bridge comes to a complete stop. What is the purpose of this bridge? Is it to save the tree by going over it? The absurdity of Armajani's project stirs up many possible readings, from gently mocking art that takes itself too seriously to acknowledging mankind's blinkered vision. I think one important way to understand *Bridge Over Tree* can be gleaned from a statement Martin Heidegger made in his essay *Building Dwelling Thinking* (1951), which was one of the inspirations for Armajani's project of architectural models, *Dictionary for Building*:

> Mortals dwell in that they save the earth—taking the word in the old sense still known to [Gotthold Ephraim] Lessing. Saving does not only snatch something from a danger. To save properly means to set something free into its own essence. To save the earth is more than to exploit it or even wear it out. Saving the earth does not master the earth and does not subjugate it, which is merely one step from boundless spoliation.[1]

In *Dictionary for Building,* which is a large, meandering body of work, Armajani ruminates over a problem that Heidegger explores in his essay: what is the relationship between the words *building* and *dwelling*?

In *Bridge Over Tree* and *Irene Hixon Whitney Bridge,* Armajani reveals his willingness to explore Heidegger's sense of *dwelling* and *saving* for the good of the earth and of the community. This understanding of *saving* is one of the motivating impulses in Armajani's thinking about the relationship between art and community, as the *Irene Hixon Whitney Bridge* makes art accessible to the urban population of Minneapolis by giving them an easy way to reach it.

Armajani has dedicated a number of works to anarchists, poets, and philosophers, as well as made an anti-war sculpture, *Fallujah* (2004), in response to the American invasion of Iraq. He also commissioned his friend, the poet John Ashbery, to write a poem for the *Irene Hixon Whitney Bridge* project. Not surprisingly, Ashbery's untitled prose poem is full of opaque sentences, at once fragmentary and self-contained. Seen as raised metal letters, the lines are found on different architectural elements of the bridge.

Depending on where we have stopped while crossing the bridge, or in which direction we are looking, we might read, "This far, it is fair to be crossing/to have crossed," or "Driving us to say what we are thinking," or "Not a conduit (confluence?) but a place." In these lines, Ashbery invites the individual to consider the relationship between language and experience, and to further ruminate on how the experience of crossing an urban bridge passing over multiple lanes of traffic might be emblematic of something else. If the bridge isn't a "conduit (confluence) but a place," how might we see it differently? Have we categorized certain parts of our daily life so that we no longer actually experience them? Has an experience such as walking over a bridge lost all sense of wonder and history for us?

The multiple functions and evocations that we find in Armajani's works stem from his conviction that art must serve a purpose, even if only as an ornament that enhances the individual's life. And yet, in contrast to the belief that ornament is extraneous, Armajani believes it is fundamental. This understanding of the relationship between ornament and function has its roots in the artist's childhood and upbringing. Born in Tehran, Iran, in 1939, Armajani has often recounted that he grew up in a house full of books and fell in love with poetry at an early age. In 1960, during pro-democracy protests against the shah, and with his father understandably worried about his politically active son, Armajani enrolled in Macalester College in St. Paul, Minnesota, where he would go on to study philosophy. Ever since he was a student, Armajani has made his home base in Minneapolis. And yet, even while living and working in the American Midwest for nearly sixty years, Armajani carries with him an awareness that in Islamic art, which is almost completely nonfigurative, the calligraphic inscriptions seen as inlaid tiles in a mosaic, for example, serve a variety of purposes—as ornament and prayer, proverb or instruction. This is different from the inscriptions we see on the bases of statues, telling us who is being memorialized and why.

In *Hall Mirror with Table* (1983–84), which is made of bronze, mirror, and painted wood, Armajani layered words into the metal frame that surrounds the table and mirror. The words, based on Ralph Waldo Emerson's writing in "Art," Essay XII (1841), read:

> If history were truly told if life were nobly spent it would be no longer easy or possible to distinguish the fine arts from
> The useful arts it is its instinct to find beauty in new and necessary facts in the field and road-side in the shop and mill.[2]

Armajani set the two layers of cut-out letters in an open, trough-like frame that forms a metaphorical window-doorway. The top, smaller layer of words is green, while the bottom, larger layer is golden-bronze, the same color as the structure. Along the top of the frame, we read the green letters "IF HISTORY . . ." Armajani is inviting the viewer to reconsider the nature of history: Can it be told "truly"? Can one's life be "nobly spent"? Can life and aesthetic appreciation merge so that the "fine arts" and the "useful arts" are one? This strikes me as the creed Armajani chooses to live by, as exemplified by the *Irene Hixon Whitney Bridge*. It is what guides his choice of projects, as well as motivates his decisions. He is not interested in art for art's sake or in making work in which the content is purely social or political.

Behind the structure, as well as framed by it, viewers see a table and mirror. We are not meant to merely examine our appearance in the hallway mirror before stepping out into the world. Rather, Armajani is asking us to think about the way we exist in the world and how we think of the objects around us. Are they there only because of their function? Is it because we think they are beautiful? Beyond their immediate purpose, what role do they have in our lives?

If the transcendental optimism of Emerson was a source for *Hall Mirror with Table* and other works, Armajani's *Edgar Allan Poe's Study* (2008), a large, glassed-in, elevated room, the entrance to which is locked by a shut gate, might seem the opposite. Denied entrance, we become estranged voyeurs staring into, as well as walking around, a glassed-in room, which is divided in half by a muslin sheet on which we see three silhouettes of a raven. In one half of this divided room, there is a green painted wooden chair with a coat hanging on the back of it. Poe has left the room, and there is no sense of when or if he might return.

And yet, before we conclude that Edgar Allan Poe's dark tales of claustrophobia and isolation are evoked as the opposite of Emerson's buoyancy, I would remind the viewer of what Poe, the author of "The Raven" and "The Fall of the House of Usher," wrote in his essay "Philosophy of Composition" (1846):

> When, indeed, men speak of Beauty, they mean, precisely, not a quality, as is supposed, but an effect—they refer, in short, just to that intense and pure elevation of soul—*not* of intellect, or of heart—upon which I have commented, and which is experienced in consequence of contemplating 'the beautiful.'

The contemplation of the beautiful is what Armajani seems to me to be after in all of his work, not as a "quality," but as "an effect." Each of the distinct (but joined) structures in *Irene Hixon Whitney Bridge* embodies a moment in which the beauty of a particular design might remind us that the world need not always be driven by material greed. Armajani's bridge joins a sculpture garden (art) to a city park (play and recreation). In his design he takes into account different kinds of experience, from seeing the bridge (and its whimsical but sturdy joinings) from a moving vehicle to walking across it and reflecting upon Ashbery's lines (when we encounter them) while looking at the changing urban vista. If we are open to it, Armajani slows down our passage across the bridge by inviting us (through the placement of lines from Ashbery's poem) to look at the constantly changing world. Will it "[drive] us to say what we are thinking"?

We might also remember that Poe was a writer who—for all of his inventive creepiness and morbidity—was focused on writing accessible tales: he wanted to reach people, even if what he delivered was unsettling.

How T. C. Cannon Redefined Native American Identity

I WONDER HOW MANY Americans know that forty-two thousand Native Americans were members of the US armed forces during the Vietnam War (1964–75), or that one in sixty-five soldiers who fought in the war was Native American. This fact leapt out at me while I was reading the wall texts in the exhibition *T. C. Cannon: At the Edge of America* at the National Museum of the American Indian (2019). Originating at the Peabody Essex Museum in Salem, Massachusetts, and movingly organized by Karen Kramer, the museum's curator of Native American and oceanic art, it is an extensive survey of the work of a wildly prolific, diverse, and brilliantly adventuresome artist who died in a car accident at the age of thirty-one.

In addition to a large number of paintings—many of which should be better known than they are—the exhibition includes drawings, sketchbooks, prints, tapes of Cannon singing his favorite songs as well as ones he wrote, poems, letters, film clips, and much else. With this range of materials, Kramer attempts to get at the often-contradictory and complex strands that wove through Cannon's brief life.

T. C. Cannon (or Tommy Wayne Cannon, 1946–78, Caddo/Kiowa) belongs to that category of doomed artists who died young. Other such artists include Frédéric Bazile (1841–70), Vincent van Gogh (1853–90), Franz Marc (1880–1916), and, closer to home,

Jean-Michel Basquiat (1960–88). All of them left us with an unquenchable desire for more.

Cannon was born in Lawton, Oklahoma, which is located in the state's southwest corner less than one hundred miles from Oklahoma City. Founded at the turn of the twentieth century on the former reservation lands of the Kiowa, Commanche, and Apache tribes, Lawton is close to Fort Sill, an army base built during the Indian Wars and still active today. Instead of trying to assimilate or deny his heritage, Cannon registered himself with his father's tribe as a Kiowa with the name Pai-doung-u-day, which translates as "one who stands in the sun."

In 1964, he enrolled in the Institute of American Indian Arts in Santa Fe, New Mexico, where he studied with, and soon influenced, Fritz Scholder, who refused to address his own Native American identity until he met Cannon. Scholder subsequently gained attention for his Expressionist portraits, which undermine stereotypes by portraying men in feathered headdress drinking a beer or sitting with an American flag in the background

Cannon was not interested in replicating stereotypes but in pursuing the possibilities of self-representation; he was determined to address the complexities and conflicts of being a member of a proud, persecuted people, whose traditions were systematically misunderstood, parodied, and outlawed during his lifetime. He wanted to make art that pushed back against the genocidal policies and relentless displacement that Native Americans have endured in the United States, a society that—unable to recognize them as individuals—simultaneously mythologizes and debases them.

In 1967, Cannon dropped out of the San Francisco Art Institute and became a paratrooper in the 101st Airborne Division. Two years later, having completed one tour and received many commendations and medals, including two Bronze Stars, he returned to civilian life. What makes Cannon's decision to join the combat especially confounding is that Cannon's favorite musician at the time was Bob Dylan, whose lyrics about the injustice of America inspired Cannon to write his own. Think about this for a moment. Cannon, a young man with immense artistic talent, who plays a guitar and writes songs and poems, decides to become a paratrooper for a country that destroyed his culture. This isn't ironic. It's tragic.

In the painting *Soldier* (1970), completed before he was twenty-five, Cannon depicts a figure with arms outstretched, in a pose that evokes a crucifixion, against a white background. The left side of the figure is red-skinned and dressed in Native American garb, while the right side is blond and fair in a blue cavalry uniform.

In another piece, the words "Minnesota Sioux" appear at the top of an ink drawing dating from the 1970s. Below, Cannon has drawn a noose with the phrase "Insert Here" beside it. As the wall text states:

> In December 1862, President Abraham Lincoln approved the executions of thirty-eight [men] in a quickly moving, unfair trial. The Dakotas were hanged a week before Lincoln's Emancipation Proclamation freed African American slaves.

John Wayne's Bullet (1973) is an ink drawing of a Native American lying horizontally. His head is raised as he looks down at his body. A fountain of blood, painted in bright red watercolor, erupts from his torso. This matter-of-fact view of Hollywood's characterization of an Indian is stinging. It recalls that oft-repeated movie line: "The only good injun is a dead one."

Cannon's greatest achievements are his painted portraits. The painting *Indian with Beaded Headdress* (1978), done the year of his death, depicts a man in ceremonial regalia. Seated sideways in an aluminum chair, with his head turned, he stares sternly and reticently at the viewer. In these and other paintings done during the 1970s, Cannon hits his stride. His subject is the dilemma that Native Americans have long faced: which customs do you hold onto and which do you relinquish? This is not a matter of identity politics but of the layers of denial and contradictions of self-representation in a society that valorizes assimilation and whiteness. How do you regain your pride?

Highly conscious of the representation of Native Americans by Edward S. Curtis, whose staged photographs ignore the sanctioned genocidal destruction that killed off more than four fifths of all Native peoples starting in 1492, Cannon restates the pose of a well-known sepia photograph by Curtis in his painting *Small Catcher* (1973–78). This painting exemplifies his directed engagement with history and representation, which is where he reaches something powerful and all his own. The paintings from this decade form a singular body of work that needs to be far better known.

And then—like a bright candle—Cannon was extinguished, leaving us with the unmistakable sense that an even more commanding greatness might have awaited him.

What's in a Name?

(on James Luna)

MORE THAN TWENTY years ago—on April 2, 1991, to be exact—James Luna (1950–2018) stood on a platform in the Whitney Museum of American Art, Downtown at Federal Reserve Plaza, and invited members of the audience to join him by announcing:

> Take a picture with a real Indian.
> Take a picture, here tonight in New York City,
> Take two. Leave one. Take one home.
> America loves to say "our Indians,"
> America likes to name cars and trucks after our tribes
> and people.
> America doesn't know me.
> Take a picture with a real Indian.
> Take a picture tonight, free.

A short distance in front of the platform, which was flanked by three cutouts of Luna (wearing a breechcloth in two and a short sleeve pullover shirt and beige pants in the third), a photographer with a Polaroid instant camera and a tripod-mounted camera waited to photograph whoever chose to join Luna.

From what I can gather, two shots were taken with Polaroid instant cameras, while another camera documented the performance, including members of the audience, in black and white, and a video camera recorded the entire event.

The props used in this performance, along with a sampling of the photographs and videos, were presented in the exhibition *James Luna: Take a Picture with a Real Indian* at Garth Greenan Gallery (2020), the first exhibition since the artist's death.

In addition to artifacts, photographs, and videos from that fabled performance, the gallery presented two sets of three large-scale photographs from Luna's series *Half Indian/Half Mexican* (1991 and 2010), one in black and white and the other in color. The proximity of these projects underscores Luna's preoccupation with identity.

Of Payómkawichum, Ipi, and Mexican American descent, he explored how he was seen in *Half Indian/Half Mexican*. Each series consists of three views of Luna: right profile, frontal, and left profile.

In the color set, which is dated 2010 and echoes the earlier black-and-white series, the leftmost photograph shows him in profile, facing to the right; his face is clean shaven, and his shoulder-length, salt-and-pepper hair is tucked behind his ear. The profile shot of his left side shows him with the beard and mustache, and his hair combed so that it does not hang down. In the frontal view his visage is split between the two looks.

The profile shots, each literally showing a different side of Luna's face, look impassively at the middle image of his partially shaven face.

I moved a chair placed in front of the platform with the three cutouts of Luna to sit with these photographs. I suppose part of it has to do with being biracial, with having a father who was half-English and half-Chinese, and being mistaken for other ethnicities throughout my life, but I don't think that was the only reason I sat in front of these photographs for a long time, reflecting upon what I saw: a man looking at his mixed identity from two different perspectives.

The division in Luna's face stirred up so many feelings I have had about the emphasis America places on identity and the abhorrence I have felt in my life about claims to racial purity and assimilation—and the judgments made solely on the basis of the way someone looks. I hardly think I am alone in this.

Luna was preoccupied with self-presentation in a society that, in its pursuit of whiteness, has never been able to recognize Native Americans as individuals, choosing either to invent or demean them. The art world is not free from this onerous behavior.

One only has to look at Andy Warhol's portfolio of ten prints, *Cowboys and Indians* (1986), which includes images of John Wayne, Annie Oakley, and President Theodore Roosevelt, alongside General George Armstrong Custer, to see how deeply imbedded America's denial of the genocidal destruction of Native Americans remains to its self-image.

Instead of doing any real research into the subject, Warhol took photographs of artifacts in the National Museum of the American Indian, New York, and paired them with mass media images. Long interested in surfaces, Warhol, in this project, arrived at something that was superficial and lazy.

In his performance *Take a Picture with a Real Indian* (1991), Luna directly challenges this widespread denial, as he makes the viewer complicit, as both participant and witness.

As with *Half Indian/Half Mexican,* I was riveted by the video clips of what happened at Luna's carefully staged, seemingly casual performance. The fact that the performance was spread across three monitors made it difficult to see the entire spectacle; my attention shifted (as it might have had I been there) from one incident to another.

This was Luna's genius; he consistently made work that cut through America's refusal of Native American self-representation, while, at the same time, exposing the nation's ugly, deeply ingrained history and perpetuating mechanisms, from the names of sports teams and logos to, as he said in his performance, the "names of cars and trucks." He did this with an unrivaled economy, and by pulling the audience in and making them participants.

I kept wondering what the people who stood next to Luna and got their photo taken would have said about the experience. Was it just a fun thing to do at an art event? Or was it more than that? Did the participants learn anything from the experience? Did they think about it later, as time passed? What about the families? That's really what held my attention—seeing parents and children standing beside Luna, as if he were an object, which in some sense he was. I admit, I could not stop looking and wondering.

Ideally, the Whitney Museum, which hosted this performance, would add it to their collection and periodically exhibit it in the museum lobby.

Even though years have passed since Luna walked through the audience, said the words I cited at the beginning of this review, and climbed onto the platform, it spoke directly to me and, I would like to think, to anyone who sat down and opened up to what they saw.

Jack Whitten's Walls

Born in Bessemer, Alabama, in 1939—during the Jim Crow era when rigid segregation was in effect—Jack Whitten belongs to the generation of abstract artists that emerged in the early 1970s, more than a decade after Minimalism, Pop Art, and Color Field first came on the scene. If we take a generation to mean about five years, then Mary Heilmann (b. 1940), Elizabeth Murray (1940–2007), and Thomas Nozkowski (b. 1944) also belong to this generation. I mention these three artists because each of them hit their stride in the 1970s, or after the 1960s, when, according to Douglas Crimp in his essay "The End of Painting" (1981), "painting's terminal condition finally seemed impossible to ignore. The symptoms were everywhere . . ."

While all four artists are innovators, Whitten is the most relentless experimenter with materials in a generation of abstract artists who have yet to receive their due, perhaps because no one has come up with a catchy and marketable name for them, like the Minimalists or the Pictures Generation. By materials, I do not just mean paint. Whitten has also used Styrofoam, hair, eggshells, molasses, copper, and coal ash in his works.

Whitten's preoccupation with experimentation has deep roots in his experience. In an interview with Kenneth Goldsmith that appeared in *BOMB* (Summer 1994), Whitten stated:

> I'm convinced today that a lot of my attitudes toward painting and making, and experimentation came from George Washington Carver. He made his own pigments, his own paints, from his inventions with peanuts. The obsession with invention and discovery impressed me.

One other thing Whitten said to Goldsmith seems particularly relevant:

> It took twenty years to get into a position where I could work myself out of history. Every painter wants to escape art history. And now there's a curve that's leading me out. My emphasis on pop culture, video, science, on the urban environment, and everything on up to the Big Bang theory excites me. I see that as a way, using those metaphors, that I can escape art historical references.

These were not the first thoughts that I had when I went to see the exhibition *Jack Whitten* at Hauser & Wirth (2017) the artist's first with this international gallery. My first response was luscious perplexity, which only the very best artists are able to swiftly induce in viewers. How does one visually account for this work and all its contradictions?

The first paintings to greet the view belong to the series *The Portals*. While the three similarly sized paintings share the same format of a circle floating inside a square, their materiality and the process by which they were made distinguishes them. They are not variations on a theme, but distinct works within a series. Whitten works magic with acrylic: he can get it to look like a polished slice of stone, a sheet of rumpled industrial plastic, or the pitted surface of a moon seen through a powerful telescope.

Whereas the circle and the title suggest a doorway or an opening, the dense material surface of the circle contradicts this. The opposition between opening and solid barrier became more apparent as I moved closer to the painting: no one achieves a surface like Whitten. In *The Third Portal* (2016), he has filled the area around the solid black circle's uneven surface with tiny, glittering, mosaic-like pieces. Other bits of color and light are scattered throughout the deep blue bricks. The bricks are made of paint that has been cast and cut, but they do not come across as machine produced.

Since the early 1970s, Whitten has been a process painter, inventing a variety of ways to start and complete a painting. In his paintings from the 1970s, he used various homemade and repurposed devices to pull acrylic paint across the painting's surface. There was a feeling of speed, of looking at something that was blurred, at a frozen motion. In the paintings in this show in which Whitten filled the surface with his cast bricks, I had the feeling that the artist was slowing down time—that the joy he gets from making these paintings is of a different nature than what he experienced in his earlier work. The other thing that strikes me about the paintings, particularly the ones from his series of *Quantum Walls,* is the way he brings together matter and immateriality, the visceral and invisible.

The spectrum of experience in these paintings is vast. One can stand at the far end of this spacious gallery and, as you walk closer to the painting, something happens at every step. First there is this ghostly apparition (or discoloration) on the painting's faceted surface. It hovers between legibility and illegibility. In the largely violet *Quantum Wall, III (The Geometry of Being an Octopus)* (2016), the darker shades of black and violet "staining" the wall appear to be on the verge of coalescing into an image but never do. Whitten seems to be getting at our desire to see, particularly in the realm of science, and how our expectations can never be met. For each thing we learn leads to more questions for which we do not have the answers. It is as if Whitten's "walls" underscore the physical limit of our perceptions, while the "stains" on them remind us that much of reality exists beyond our grasp.

The conversation Whitten establishes between visibility and invisibility goes in myriad directions—from social matters of race to philosophical and scientific speculations about the nature of the universe. At the same time, Whitten's walls evoke the invisible and forgotten laborer. His masonry of cast paint evokes the anonymous laborers who built the Americas, from those who inlaid the Mayan mosaics to the slaves who built the White House, from the bricklayers who colored the mortar the way Frank Lloyd Wright wanted to the welders who erected Santiago Calatrava's transit hub in Lower Manhattan. By making work that shares something with the constructions of anonymous laborers, Whitten reminds us that there is more to art making than fabrication or craftsmanship. Moreover, the world is not divided just into employer and employee, which is a model in need of serious revision. Whitten's art is a challenge to mainstream thinking on many different levels, from the relationship of subject matter to abstraction to the connection between art making and art. Isn't it time to acknowledge these challenges? Abstract art did not culminate in the 1960s, and it is about time we got around to embracing that fact, and not what art world institutions and various authorities have repeatedly tried to foist on us.

Demotic Abstraction

(on Barbara Takenaga)

SINCE THE BEGINNING of this century, painter Barbara Takenaga has slowly expanded her creative process, moving from a set structure, which she explored, to an open-ended procedure in which meticulous control and the surrender of power interact with one another—with unexpected results. While she was doing this, she was also enlarging her vocabulary to include Japanese symbols, such as a pattern of fish-scale lines, into her work. Another image resembles a geyser of steam rising into the air, its base framed by concentric rings punctuated by dots.

By concentrating on detail, which is a central feature of Takenaga's work, she has gone against the reductive tendencies of Minimalism that still haunt painting. In her earlier work, she incorporated her details within all-over compositions, making them part of a larger, highly orchestrated field. Over the past few years, and particularly in her exhibition, *Barbara Takenaga: Outset* at DC Moore Gallery (2018), the artist has moved into a fresh territory. She has transformed the roots of her work (graphic art and the Pattern and Decoration movement) into something in which repetition has broken free.

This means that Takenaga has become more focused on composition. Her recurring subject is a view of nature that is simultaneously real and imagined. In *Serrulata* (2018), the artist layers multiple vocabularies and processes—patterns, pours, splotches, and drips—without trying to order them into an all-over composition. The palette is composed of contrasts—dark blues, blacks, and grays—that further compress the layered space in which different kinds of marks are pressed together. Instead of being soothed by repetition, we are given disruption. *Serrulata,* the painting's title, is another name for the Japanese cherry tree, which is central to the spring cherry blossom festival. The pink flowers blossom for about two weeks before falling; the transience of their beauty is a reminder of life's brevity.

By working with blacks and dark blues, Takenaga resists the inherent beauty of the festival's colors. The different vocabularies that she brings together—a repeated arch and the drop of black paint spreading on the painting's surface—evoke order, repetition, dispersal, and decay. The lack of a determining, overall pattern enhances our experience of looking at the painting; we get lost in it, perhaps scrutinizing only a small part. We will likely enter into the painting differently the next time we look closely. The black drops that are spread unevenly across the surface also suggest, to me, the vulnerability of art—that it, too, is subject to nature. I was reminded of the beauty one finds in damaged works.

In other paintings, such as *The Edge* (2018), she evokes meteor showers. What gives Takenaga's work a deeper resonance than one encounters in much contemporary abstraction is her allusion to a world under constant pressure and in a state of unabated change. I'm also struck by the work's overt visual appeal. A field full of beaded lines going in multiple directions simultaneously is visually sensual. Meticulousness and pleasure meet in these marks. It is clear the artist is attentive to each shift in direction, as none of the rhythmic lines repeat themselves. The dance between order and individuation is precise and exquisite. The vastness of space embraced by *The Edge* conveys the possibility of solace in this time of terror and disruption.

Manifold 5 (2018) is a five-panel painting possibly inspired by Japanese screens. In her catalog essay for this exhibition, Lily Wei states: "Some of the shapes in these paintings are silhouetted abstractions of imagery taken from *byobu* (Japanese folding screens) and traditional Asian paintings."

The palette is largely black and silver. What Takenaga has absorbed and transformed into her own is the combination of austerity and lustrousness that one finds in Japanese screens. In *Manifold 5*, a black curved (or phallic) shape occupies the central three panels, framed by a silvery phallic shape entering in from the painting's right side and a silvery, largely monochromatic panel on the far left. There are numerous geysers spread across the black-and-silver shapes, suggesting another world that exists beneath the surface. A web of blues lines that shifts from fish scale to grid also demarcates the black shape. In places the silver surface seems to be in a state of decay. Again, what Takenaga is able to do is use the details of a painting—be it a painterly incident or an image—to inflect the entire composition, add a different note of feeling.

By moving from an emphasis on all-over compositions, guided by repetition, to a focus on the possibilities inherent in the details, and by merging her penchant for scrupulous devotion to an acceptance of chance, Takenaga has pushed her work into a territory all her own. In this show—which ranges from large, multipanel works to ones you can hold in your hand—what impressed me most were the different vocabularies she had gathered together, from images and patterns inspired by Japanese art to natural forms seen under a microscope to tight patterns derived from fractals. Images and processes derived from biology, mathematics, and astronomy mixed with classical Japanese art and midcentury abstraction add up to a heady mixture. What offsets it all is the democratic impulse running through all her work, a commitment to the possibilities of a high-minded visual pleasure that anyone can enjoy.

VI.

Kerry James Marshall's Sense of History

On November 7, 2016, *New Yorker* art critic Peter Schjeldahl concluded his review of *Kerry James Marshall: Mastry* at The Met Breuer on an optimistic note:

> There have been other significant African-American painters in recent years, including Robert Colescott, whose somewhat similar engagement with art history ran to fantasias of interracial romance, and Jean-Michel Basquiat, whose linear panache qualified him as the greatest of American neo-expressionists. But Marshall's "Mastry" has a breakthrough feel: the suggestion of a new normal, in art and in the national consciousness.

Two days later, after the election results began appearing on screens all across America, it was clear that the old normal had replaced the "new normal," that whatever "breakthrough feel" existed before election day had been halted in its tracks, that the days of terror and fear were going to begin again, not that they ever went away for many people. It is this fear—as well as happiness, desire, love, anger, remembrance, and frustration—that Marshall grapples with in his work. What he possesses is an ability to render a wide range of complex and even contradictory feelings into paint—to be simultaneously intricate, nuanced, mysterious, unsettling, and direct.

Kerry James Marshall was born in Birmingham, Alabama, in 1955, one year after the Supreme Court overruled the Plessy vs. Ferguson decision—which upheld state segregation laws—by awarding a victory for the civil rights of African Americans in Brown vs. the Board of Education. The Court ruled in 1954 that separate but equal is not equal, which offered many people hope for the first time. In 1963, the artist's family moved to Watts for a year before moving to South Central, Los Angeles. The Watts Uprising began on August 11, 1965—in response to what inhabitants recognized was the latest incidence of police brutality—and lasted five days. Thirty-four people died.

In 1965, when he was ten, Marshall went to the Los Angeles County Museum for the first time. This is how he remembered it, in a quotation from the Schjeldahl article:

> I went from floor to floor looking at everything, in the same way that in the library I went down the stacks and looked at every art book, without discrimination.

Marshall soaked it all up, at once innocent and hungry. One lesson he took away from this experience was that there were no paintings of Black people on the museum's walls, and that realization has driven his work. No one he saw looked remotely like him, a situation that he has dedicated his life to rectifying. This story, which is known by anyone who has more than a passing familiarity with Marshall's work, bears retelling.

One reason it needs to be retold is that at the time when Marshall painted *A Portrait of the Artist as a Shadow of His Former Self* (1980) in egg tempera, a medium that historically preceded oil painting, many white critics had proclaimed that painting was dead. The painting measures eight by six-and-a-half inches, making many of the large Neo-Expressionist paintings done in these years look overblown and pompous. Inspired by Ralph Ellison's novel *Invisible Man* (1952), in which the unnamed Black narrator, who recognizes that he is invisible, states:

> My task was one of revealing the human universals hidden within the plight of one who was both Black and American.

This is the project that Marshall set for himself. Like Ellison, who did not think of the *Invisible Man* as a protest novel, Marshall is interested in the nuances of invisibility, in how much goes unseen, and the many different ways willful blindness manifests itself. In *A Portrait of the Artist as a Shadow of His Former Self*, Marshall limits his palette to blacks and grays, except for the whites of his eyes and his teeth, one of which is missing. This face looms in the darkness, almost ready to disappear back into it. This is a portrait of the Black man as caricature, which is a kind of shadow. As to his former self, what happened to it? Or has it, in the age of the death of the author and the self, become a permanent absence to be replaced only by caricature, parody, and citation? How do you cite a Black body if there is none to be found? In *Portrait of the Artist & a Vacuum* (1981), he depicts his portrait alone on a red wall behind an unplugged vacuum cleaner, evoking the long history of people of color working to maintain someone else's home. And yet, the presence of the portrait leaves open the question: whose home is it?

In the paintings done around 1990, many with collage elements and writing, Marshall is drawing on a wide range of sources, from Byzantine icons to Frida Kahlo and Mexican retablos. In *When Frustration Threatens Desire* (1990), Marshall depicts a Black man in a suit and vest with his arms extended, while beneath them floats a Black woman in a white gauzy dress. Look at the delicate lines of the gauze, and then look at the way he paints the black cat—a reference to the cat in Edouard Manet's *Olympia* (1863). The painting is replete with references to cabalistic symbols, Haitian Voudon, Santeria, and neighborhood spiritualists. In an interview with Calvin Reid that appeared in *BOMB* (Winter 1998), Marshall says about this painting:

> What also started to crystallize in that painting was a way to bring together not only Western traditions of pic-

> torial representation, but folk traditions of painting that have an equally valid authority. I don't see much difference between using Giotto or Bill Traylor as a point of reference. To me they're the same. Their work has a certain power.

I think that Marshall's equating of Giotto and Traylor is central to any understanding we have of his work. By rejecting the hierarchical thinking that establishes what is great and what's minor, which is really an academic way of dealing with the world, the kind that enabled authorities to declare painting dead, Marshall challenges and breaks down these divisions—often along racial lines—in order to move forward.

This was a big show, taking up two floors of the museum. Turn a corner and you were surprised—so much was packed into the exhibition. It included early collages, paintings, large illuminated panels from his comic strip of a black superhero, *Rythm Mastr*, an installation of his photographs, and a selection curated by the artist from the Metropolitan Museum's permanent collection titled *Kerry James Marshall Selects*—an exhibition of inspirations within a retrospective survey.

One thing missing from the show is Marshall's sculptures. I also wish there was more information and space given to the comic strip. But, in Marshall's curated selection, to see works by Charles White, Horace Pippin, Georges Seurat, Jean-Auguste-Dominique Ingres, George Tooker, Willem de Kooning, woodcuts by Yoshitoshi, photographs by Roy DeCarava, and a Senufo oracle figure in the same room—and with no hierarchy—was great. Artists—at least the ones I know and respect—don't distinguish between minor and major, self-taught or otherwise. They love art and don't focus on status or position.

In his merging of medium and subject matter, Marshall recognized that he had to insert himself into a history that was declared finished, and therefore closed off to him and to others—women and artists of color. The authorities (or are they the authoritarians?) who pronounced painting to be dead lived in a bubble: they refused to recognize how neatly the narrative they kept spinning fit into the erasures and belittlements characterizing America's modern era. This era is marked by the Dred Scott decision (1857), the Chinese Exclusion Act (1880), Plessy vs. Ferguson (1896), Hollywood's denigration of Black people and Asian people throughout its history, President Roosevelt's executive order (February 1942) ordering the relocation of all Americans of Japanese ancestry to internment camps, the Supreme Court's overruling in 2013 of key parts of the Voting Rights Act (1965), and the election of Donald J. Trump as president: white fear turned into the new normal. But what's normal for some is hell for others.

This is why Marshall's achievement is nothing short of miraculous. Amidst all the pronouncements of the death of painting, and the celebration of the latest addenda and accommodation to the narrative of painting's death, Marshall has refused to eat from the hand he has been offered. He has tackled social history, portraits, and history painting, and has concocted figures from his imagination. He doesn't sugarcoat history either. In the painting *The Actor Hezekiah Washington as Julian Carlton Taliesin Murderer of Frank Lloyd Wright Family* (2009), Marshall depicts an imaginary actor as Carlton, who murdered seven people, including Wright's mistress and her children, with a hatchet and gasoline. In this day and age, Carlton, who died of starvation while in jail awaiting trial, would be classified as a mass murderer. He never revealed why he committed the murders, and all sorts of theories have been advanced. By portraying an imaginary actor in the role of Carlton, Marshall returns to the theme of invisibility from another perspective. Can we ever know what motivated him to do this deed? And yet, Marshall affords Carlton a certain dignity and mystery: we cannot see into his angry soul nor know the source of his agitation.

In the 1990s, Marshall began painting large group portraits on unstretched canvases outfitted with grommets for hanging on the wall—complex tableaux that can be taken down and rolled up. The unstretched canvases, which remind me of tarpaulins, underscore Marshall's sense that all this might be temporary, that these paintings might soon be rolled up and put in storage.

Marshall uses three combinations of black to depict his subjects: carbon, ivory, and mars black. His characters are simultaneously actual figures and symbols, most likely because Marshall, like Ellison before him, felt that Realism was too limiting. Any truth he would get at would have to be through fiction, the fusion of something he witnessed, studied, and imagined. Marshall is a history painter but not a documentarian. His paintings are the synthesis of the actual and the imagination.

All through the '90s, Marshall turned out one majestic painting after another. Prepare to be dazzled, challenged, and disturbed. Marshall can be tender and sweet; he can memorialize the dead (from children to presidents and Civil Rights leaders); he can praise beauty and rewrite history; he can evoke histories and events that have been neglected or glossed over; he can be sardonic; he can evoke fear and embrace anger; and he can be enigmatic. At no point did I feel that he was calling attention to himself or saying, I suffered or felt this. If anything, Marshall has found ways to expand his subjectivity and memories so that the self takes at least one step back. In contrast to Walt Whitman, he embraces multitudes without using "I." This is what he shares with the great figurative painters, starting with Jean-Auguste-Dominique Ingres and Franz Hals, and including Manet, Georges Seurat, Paula Modersohn-Becker, Frida Kahlo, Jacob Lawrence, Horace Pippin, and Willem de Kooning—an interest in the body, the individual, and groups.

In *De Style* (1993), a breakthrough painting which measures around ten by ten feet, Marshall depicts the interior of a neighborhood barbershop. There are three men more or less occupying the center of the painting, with rays extending out from the barber's head, suggesting that he is a saint of some sort. On the left, a woman is seated, looking out at the viewer. Her mountain of hair alludes to a traditional African style while being contemporary American at the same time. Seated next to the woman is a partially visible man, whose right hand is adorned with a sleek ring with the word "STUD" spelled out on it.

The painting's title is a reference to the stock and trade of an actual barbershop as well as a homophonic play on the Dutch utopian art movement De Stilj, which posited the use of horizontals, verticals, and elementary colors, including black and white, in search of universal principles. The barbershop's name, Percy's House of Style, is partially reflected, in reverse, in the mirror behind the barber, where we also find a master's certificate issued by the Mid-City Barber's College. This is a world—from the partially visible photograph of the boxer Joe Louis, nicknamed the Brown Bomber to the flyer for "Super Groom" to the "style guide" of head shots behind the Zenith radio—where no white people are present, and, more importantly, where none of the inhabitants seem the least bit concerned about this. The shallow space and the placement of the bodies within it deliberately links the painting to Rembrandt's *The Syndics of the Drapers' Guild* (1662), his first and only corporate group portrait, while the use of red, white, and two shades of blue (along with the painting's title) alludes to Piet Mondrian and Theo van Doesburg and the beginnings of Dutch modernism, as well as the American flag. Rather than looking back, or being wistful or ironic, Marshall synthesizes these precedents, bringing them into the present. In contrast to Rembrandt's painting, which depicts only men in the group, Marshall includes a woman in his gathering. Nothing is frozen, and everything can change and be revised. This means that painting isn't dead or even exhausted. Until the art world recognizes that, it will still place Marshall in a special category, and frankly that's ridiculous and even racist. He increases our understanding of what painting can do.

Marshall's love of detail, no matter how banal, animates his paintings. From the poster of Chris Offili's exhibition at the Tate, to the paint-covered sign welcoming people to a housing project, to song lyrics unfurling across the painting's surface, to the wallpaper, furniture, and decorative pottery, to an oversized painter's palette, to the bloodied head of a white man lying on a pillow—everything feels urgent and necessary. When Marshall includes an unfinished "paint by numbers" portrait being worked on by an imagined Black artist, he quietly reminds us that these popular sets were pitched to the white consumer. For that company, people of color did not exist. If you think that such an absence had no effect on children growing up in America in the fifties through the seventies, I can tell you from experience that you are wrong. And if you think that such oversights are gone, think about the casting of Scarlett Johansson as Major Motoko Kusanagi in the movie *Ghost in the Shell*. My fifteen-year-old and their friends have.

While many writers have praised Marshall's "Garden" paintings, which they certainly deserve, I want to call attention to two works that have gained less attention: *Black Painting* (2003-2006) and *Red (If They Come in the Morning)* (2011). In the abstract *Red (If They Come in the Morning)*, Marshall recasts Barnett Newman's painting *Who's Afraid of Red, Yellow and Blue III* (1967), one of four paintings he did with that title between 1966 and 1970. Marshall's painting, which measures eight feet by more than seventeen feet, is done in black, red, and green, the colors of the Pan-African flag, which was created by Marcus Garvey and members of the UNIA (Universal Negro Improvement Association). The colors symbolize blood and sacrifice (red), the color of the people (black), and the fertility of Africa (green).

The phrase "If they come in the morning," which is barely visible, is written in different shades of red on the red ground that takes up most of the painting. The words emerge out of the red as well as sink back into it. The line is a rephrasing of a closing line from an open letter that James Baldwin wrote to Angela Davis while she was in jail, accused of aiding the prisoner George Jackson in his attempt to escape from a California courtroom. Known as the Soledad Three, Jackson, along with two other men, Fleeta Drumgo and John Clutchette, had been falsely accused of murdering a white prison guard in 1969. By inserting this sentence into Newman's well-known painting, as well as changing the colors to the Pan-African flag, Marshall underscores the divisions in America. Newman, who identified himself as an anarchist, made paintings that denied space, figuration, gesture, and painterly incident. They were visceral feats of pure opticality. It seems to me that their vulnerability is also part of their meaning. Critics define Newman's works as art about art, attempts at attaining pure objectivity. They are regarded as a culmination.

Jackson, who became a member of the Black Panther Party while in prison, was shot to death in prison on August 21, 1970, about six weeks after Newman had died on July 4, 1970. It was his second escape attempt. Davis was accused of aiding him in the first attempt and imprisoned for eighteen months until she was found innocent. I am sure Marshall knows all this and much more. By making Baldwin's chilling words inhabit Newman's painting, Marshall rejects the ideals associated with art about art: he presents a counter narrative, which starts with *Portrait of the Artist as a Shadow of His Former Self* (1980) and continues to the present. I don't think he is asking us to take sides. Rather, he is asking us to consider the merits of two histories and their parallel existence. I would venture that by opening Newman's painting back up, by literally and metaphorically inserting himself into it, he is challenging those who uphold the narrative that painting is dead, that it culminated in the silkscreens of Andy Warhol, or that it was superseded by the stripes of Daniel Buren. In his work, Marshall is claiming that it is possible to move painting forward by opening it up to the history it ignored.

It took me a long time to see *Black Painting*, which is Marshall's redoing of a black painting by Ad Reinhardt. Once our eyes adjust, we recognize that we are standing on the edge of a bedroom with no lights. The flag of the Black Panthers is discernible in the upper right-hand corner, above a dresser. There are two people in the bed, a man and a woman: we are in the same room as Fred Hampton and his girlfriend, Deborah Johnson (also known as Akua Njeri), who is eight-and-a-half months pregnant. In a few minutes the Chicago police will burst through the door with guns blazing. Two people will be killed, Fred Hampton and Mark Clark, who was standing guard outside the room.

This is what actually happened: On December 4, 1969, the Chicago police assassinated Hampton, who had been slipped barbiturates by an FBI informant. The crime scene was tampered with and the police involved lied, claiming the Panthers had been "vicious" and "violent," none of which was true. At the same time, the FBI, under the orders of J. Edgar Hoover, was using a concerted program of disinformation to sow discord between various groups, including the Black Panthers, Young Lords, and Students for a Democratic Society. It wasn't divide and conquer so much as divide and destroy. Who is to say it cannot happen again? Or that it isn't still going on?

In 1970, a lawsuit was filed on Hampton and Clark's behalf. In 1982, a settlement of 1.85 million dollars was reached with the families of Hampton and Clark. Without any of the officials involved going to jail, the city of Chicago admitted guilt and gave the families money. This is the American way. It is called whitewashing.

When President-elect Donald Trump appointed Stephen Bannon—Breitbart executive and master of disinformation—to be his chief White House strategist and senior counselor, I wondered if Marshall's re-envisioning of Hampton's assassination was a prelude to the new normal. Perhaps painting doesn't make anything happen, at least not in any direct and obvious way. But it does have the ability to celebrate, mourn, tell, and imagine the lives of Black people—among the many things that Marshall's work does—as it challenges us to open our eyes and see as deeply as we can into the darkness that is moving swiftly toward us, reaching every corner of our lives.

All the World's a Stage

The Art of Martin Wong

IN HIS AUTOBIOGRAPHICAL, trompe l'oeil painting *My Secret World, 1978–81* (1984), Martin Wong depicts a brick wall punctuated by two windows that provide a partial view of a hotel room. In the window to the left, Wong "chiseled" the room number and the hotel's address on the lintel and his name and the date the painting was completed on the sill. The lintel on the right reads: "It was in this room that the world's first paintings for the hearing impaired came into being," while the sill shows the painting's title. Despite the thoroughness of Wong's statements, the painting is not completely transparent. From our perch outside the windows, we cannot see everything in the room. Arguably, the inspiration for Wong's painting was Vincent van Gogh's painting of his bedroom in Arles. In contrast to van Gogh's intimate setting, which locates the viewer inside the room, Wong places us on the outside—we are voyeurs peering through open windows.

Through the window on the left, we see part of the artist's painting *Psychiatrists Testify: Demon Dogs Drive Man to Murder* (1980), in which a series of gesticulating hands, suspended inside a window similarly set into a brick wall, spell out the painting's title in American Sign Language (ASL). The black ground on which the gesticulating hands are depicted can be read as the night sky, transforming the hands into cosmic signs. The right border of the hotel room's left window truncates the title, which is lettered above and below the depicted hands. What we are able to read is "Psychiatrists Testify" and "Demon Dogs Drive Man."

The man in the title is the serial killer David Berkowitz (a.k.a. Son of Sam), who shot six people in New York in the summer of 1977. According to the psychiatrists who examined him, Berkowitz claimed that a dog, which had channeled the spirit of a six-thousand-year-old man, ordered him to shoot his victims. Included in the original painting, but not in Wong's painting-within-a-painting, is an additional inscription that reads, "Painting for the hearing impaired."

Wong is interested in madness and "voices" and their relationship to artists. By showing only part of the painting's title, Wong transforms a tabloid headline into something more benign, something that might be applicable to van Gogh or even Wong. Through the window on the left, we also glimpse two more paintings above the artist's neatly made bed. The one on top depicts an eight ball against a brick wall, while the bottom one shows a pair of dice, the exposed sides of each showing the sum of seven dots. Wong's images of bad luck and good luck are part of his worldview, along with his interest in different kinds of language, from the aural hallucinations of the insane to the hand signals of ASL.

Through the window on the right, we see a row of books on top of a dresser, along with a box containing an eight ball and dice, suggesting that everything Wong paints is based on something real. There are a variety of book titles: *Flying Saucers, The Universe, Pro Hockey, Pirate Stories, How to Make Money, Crossword Puzzles, Unbeatable Bruce Lee, Picture Book of Freaks,* and *Anti-Gravity*. By bookending the row with the titles *Flying Saucers* and *Anti-Gravity*, Wong reveals his determination to overcome whatever obstacles stand in his way, while also registering an array of aspirations, pursuits, and temptations, including the desire to "make money," as well as an interest in sports and sports figures (or masculinity), male adventures (pirate stories), Asian identity, and being a "freak."

As the painting's title suggests, and its format confirms, we are Peeping Toms who can glimpse only a portion of Wong's life. By turning viewers into scopophiliacs, the artist emphasizes that looking is not virtuous, and that there is no such thing as an innocent eye. Rather, there is a gap (or partial barrier) between the viewer and the viewed. Wong is positing a dilemma between telling and withholding, which lies at the heart of all art. Throughout his career, Wong found ways to both challenge and acknowledge this as well as other dilemmas and prohibitions. His highly informed fearsomeness and imaginative solutions are what I want to call attention to in this essay.

First, however, I want to establish the formal affinities he shares with two widely celebrated, highly sophisticated, self-taught artists from an earlier generation, Jasper Johns and Robert Ryman. My primary reason for doing this is to offer a fresh view of the intricate visual details that Wong is able to compress within his paintings, which range from detailed depictions of the crumbling environs of his beloved East Village to restaged views of a bygone era of San Francisco's Chinatown.

Wong is known for his, as Dan Cameron puts it, "meticulous rendering of thousands of individual bricks to produce an image of a blank wall." However, I want to advance that his seemingly obsessive attention to detail can in fact be seen in a context that connects him to Johns and Ryman. Rather than engaging in some "obsessive-compulsive method, often associated with outsider folk artists like Joseph Yoakum or Martin Ramirez" that suggests a closed, repeated approach, Wong remained open to both his everyday world and to his imagination. More than anything else, Wong's openness is what distinguishes him from folk artists. I am reminded of the poet Robert Duncan's definition of responsibility: "responsibility is to keep / the ability to respond."[1]

In contrast to those who study painting in art school and learn from their teachers what constitutes mastery, Wong, Johns, and Ryman are self-taught painters. Unlike self-taught painters such as Yoakum or Ramirez who developed an inflexible style from which they seldom ventured, Wong, Johns, and Ryman see themselves as perpetual students devoted to intensifying the possibilities of their medium. The sense of always being a student—that is, someone who keeps exploring how to make a painting because it can never be fully learned—helps explain their lifelong commitment to integrating their materials with a painstaking attention to both detail and the whole. All three artists find different ways to demonstrate that they are taking full responsibility for what they do in their art. In each case, the result is the development of a unique object, signed and dated by the artist, which invites slow and careful looking upon the part of the viewer. For what these painters ask of the viewer is a careful accounting of each aspect of their works that looks beyond the immediacy of their paintings. This parsing out mirrors the exactitude that these artists bring to their work, and their refusal to take anything for granted.

Their use of language leads to the other connection that Wong, Johns, and Ryman share. Despite the obvious differences in intention, all of them make paintings and hybrid objects in which language—be it as basic as the artist's name, the work's title, the place where it was made, and the date on which it was completed—functions as a necessary component of the composition. In their work, seeing and reading, the visual and the physical, are intertwined.

Moreover, in his intaglio diptych, *Fragment of a Letter* (2010), Johns incorporated the manual alphabet of ASL into the work, something that Wong began doing in the early 1980s. As Wong spelled out in his painting *My Secret World, 1978–81*: "It was in this room the world's first paintings for the hearing impaired came into being." Coincidentally, the letter Johns cites is from Vincent van Gogh to his friend Emile Bernard.

Johns's paintings and sculptures clearly inspired Wong throughout his career. By employing a trompe l'oeil approach to his subjects, Wong consciously connected himself to John F. Peto, who had inspired Johns, as well as embraced the challenge that such an association entailed. Here we get a glimpse of Wong's artistic ambition. In order not to be seen as derivative of Peto or Johns, Wong knew that he must make something that is recognizably his. That he was able to do so within a few years after committing himself—at the age of thirty—to being a painter is a testament to an analytic intelligence steeped in a wild imagination.

A thorough student of his precursors and a highly sophisticated artist, Wong synthesized a wide variety of sources, ranging from high art, popular culture, and Asian entertainers to personal history, family photographs, and close observation. According to Barry Blinderman, Wong's first gallery dealer, his sources include "Persian and Christian illuminated manuscripts, Chinese painting from the Sung dynasty to the present, and American folk art." This only hints at the expansiveness of Wong's visual acuity. As manifested by his collection of more than three hundred works of graffiti art, which he donated to the Museum of the City of New York in 1994—and the many other collections he assembled, including a large group of American-produced racist caricatures of Asians—Wong possessed a keen eye, a voracious appetite, and a big-hearted willingness to accept the paradoxes he encountered in his life.

Wong's scrupulousness was driven by a necessity to be true to the layered complexity of his subject matter and myriad feelings, while consciously working within the strictures brought to bear by formal reasoning. As the poet and critic Barry Schwabsky astutely points out, Wong's work is "tinged with memorializing passion that never stops to ask whether an object is real or imaginary. His peculiar and highly literate synthesis of allegorical reverie and social realism, formal concision and memorial ardor is perhaps even more poignant today than when he first attracted attention in the early eighties as part of the emerging East Village art scene."[2]

Brimming with contradictory impulses, Wong was a social realist and a visionary dreamer, a painstaking craftsman and a lover of kitsch, who could be simultaneously critical and the head of a fan club. By bringing these very different, seemingly antagonistic possibilities into play, he became an iconoclast whose legacy includes expanding the narrow, received view of the ethnic painter as the storyteller (or spokesperson) for the tribe. For one thing, Wong's tribe—the people he feels at home with and whom he chronicles—crosses racial boundaries and challenges gender stereotypes. It is a community that is simultaneously real and created.

Moreover, in his depictions of Bruce Lee, Mei Lang-Fang (a Chinese opera star famous for his female impersonations), and other Asian entertainers, Wong further complicates the viewer's understanding of ethnic and sexual identity, as well as sexual appetites, particularly as it is defined by mainstream culture. It is a complication that runs through all of Wong's work, whether the subject is Chinatown, the East Village, or his declaration of homoerotic olfactory desire in the painting *I Really Like the Way Firemen Smell* (1988).

Born in 1946 in Portland, Oregon, Wong grew up further down the coast, in San Francisco's Chinatown, which remains both a tourist destination and a tightly knit social enclave. After graduating from George Washington High School, he studied ceramics at Humboldt State. His study of ceramics would exert an immense influence on his practice as a painter, particularly on his palette (with its earth reds, burnt siennas, ochers, and umbers) and in his deep feeling for materials. His use of gold acrylic to convey the mortar between the bricks, as the outline of his figures, and to draw the stylized hand signals from the manual alphabet, recalls the transformation of glazes in the kiln as well as the transubstantiations of alchemy. The juxtaposition of an earthy palette with gold suggests that Wong believed that one can—through the medium of paint—transform lowly matter into spiritual substance.

In 1978, after living in Eureka and San Francisco for a decade, Wong moved to New York, eventually settling in the East Village, a largely Hispanic neighborhood of tenements and burned-out and abandoned buildings. As an openly gay Chinese American man, Wong was considered an outsider in this neighborhood. However, instead of trying to hide his outsider status, Wong called attention to it by wearing a cowboy hat and shirt and sporting a Fu Manchu moustache. While he taught himself Spanish and earned the nickname "Chino Malo" (Bad Chinese), he was always "unfailingly garbed in his best space-cowboy attire."[3]

In the paintings that first gained Wong attention in the short-lived East Village art scene, he incorporated the manual alphabet of ASL into compositions of constellations and tenements. As Blinderman points out, these signs suggest that the painter recognizes that he must make his hands "speak." Wong's use of the manual alphabet can be understood on a number of levels. As someone growing up in San Francisco's Chinatown, Wong was aware that language could be both a form of communication and a barrier, particularly to those who are unfamiliar with it. Moving to a neighborhood in the East Village where many residents spoke Spanish must have reinforced this early memory.[4]

Since ASL is strictly visual, Wong might have also associated it with the language of signals used by a segment of New York's gay community who wished to announce their sexual availability. It is also worth noting that *Signs of Sexual Behavior: An Introduction to Some Sex-Related Vocabulary in American Sign Language* by James Woodward was published in paperback in 1979. By using the manual alphabet to spell out words in his work, Wong recognizes that painting is a language of signs that combines the visual and physical, while acknowledging that art, no matter how accessible, is not universal. In fact, just the opposite—art must always be deciphered and interpreted. By depicting stylized versions of hand signs, Wong signals that there is a gap between the viewer (reader) and the art (signs) that the artist (messenger) must try and transcend without betraying or simplifying his subject.

In *Clones of Bruce Lee* (1981), he uses the manual alphabet to spell out the painting's title, which he places against a black ground. But without this knowledge, the viewer might associate the hand signs with Chinese ideograms. In one version of another sign language painting, *Courtroom Shocker/Jimmy the Weasel Sings Like a Canary* (1984), Wong also transcribes the painting's title, derived from a tabloid newspaper, into hand signs, which he uses to fill the painting's square format, effectively turning it into a sign. In an earlier version of the painting, Wong uses trompe l'oeil Realism to depict the same hand signs in a wood-framed painting mounted on a brick wall, a "stamped metal plate" beneath it with the headline and artist's name spelled out. Wong has interpreted the hands signs for the viewer, literally spelled out what they mean.

Within a short time after his arrival in New York, Wong was chronicling his life in the East Village, as well as that of his neighbors, friends, and lovers, against a backdrop of brick tenements, tar-covered schoolyards, graffitied walls, and abandoned buildings. Focusing on his distressed neighborhood, and its Latino and Black residents, Wong stood apart from the other artists who were also gaining attention in the East Village art scene: Keith Haring, Sherrie Levine, Kiki Smith, Philip Taaffe, and David Wojnarowicz. He was an artist of the local, chronicling the Hispanic neighborhood, as well as recording different aspects of his identity as an openly gay Chinese American with desires and memories, all of which were at odds with mainstream America. He did all this without a trace of cynicism or irony, but with noticeable sympathy, tenderness, and even innocence.

Wong lovingly painted crumbling tenement walls, one brick at a time, chain-link fences, padlocks, and shuttered steel gates. He memorialized stripped-down cars, storefront temples and churches, courtroom testimony, graffiti, poems by Miguel Piñero, and Hollywood Asians such as Bruce Lee and his television character, Kato. In his trompe l'oeil memorialization, *Pedro's Lament* (1984), as Blinderman perceptively points out, "Wong's vertiginous substitution of real objects for representations of objects, and conversely of veneer for real substance, sets up an oscillation between the realms of painting and architecture as bearers of 'stories.'"[5]

In the diptych *Flagstone Boogie Woogie* (1984), he carefully rendered rough-surfaced flagstones in homage to Piet Mondrian. He depicted Spanish, English, and Chinese store signs, the calligraphy of signage seen on walls, as well as transcribed conversations and poems into paint. He was a documentarian and a fantasist, an ardent observer and a wishful dreamer, an insider and an outsider, all of which he gets into his work. Although they might be mute witnesses, Wong's walls do "talk"—and they invite the viewer to see and listen.

By depicting his Hispanic and Black friends, lovers, and neighbors, Wong challenged the underlying assumption that ethnic painters should stick to themes approved by their own race, as well as by mainstream America. Moreover, by redefining what was possible, he opened the door for future generations. Identity was not something the individual was given, but something that was constructed, like a costume and a mask. When it came to identity, Wong was not an essentialist. In hindsight, given the racial tension and widespread homophobia in 1980s America, the wonder of Wong's work is how intrepid he was in exploring his desires and memories. He willingly defied expectations regarding ethnic storytelling in paint. Even now, what strikes me about Wong's multifaceted body of work is how courageous and adventuresome he was throughout his tragically short career, which barely spanned two decades.

Wong was fearless in his desire to get it right, to paint each brick as if his life depended on it. Despite his social realist impulses, his paintings resist any easy reading and, more importantly, are not didactic. Wong was a complex man who made intricate paintings in which a multitude of languages, from the written to the visual, both coincide and collide. By bringing together constellations (and their names), book titles, stylized hand gestures derived from ASL, words in English and Spanish, Chinese ideograms, tattoos, and graffiti, Wong recognizes that America is a multilingual country in which no language is central.

Rather than being part of a utopian "melting pot," each of us belongs to a community and speaks that group's language. Ideally, the individual who is conversant in more than one *langue de tribe* will be able to successfully move across different groups and enclaves. After growing up in San Francisco's Chinatown, studying ceramics at Humboldt State, living in the town of Eureka, being an active member of the hippie community in Haight Ashbury, and electing to be openly gay, Wong had to have been aware of many distinct signifying systems, or what Ferdinand de Saussure called *langue* (language) and *parole* (speaking). It is his inclusiveness that sets Wong apart from his contemporaries.

In Wong's paintings, America (as represented by the East Village and Chinatown, both in New York and San Francisco) comes across as a decaying world in which many secret and coded languages are used. While some observers may connect the coded languages to Wong's gay identity, it also has to do with being Chinese American, and growing up in a tightly knit neighborhood where more than one language was in constant use. This dual consciousness of language was deeply ingrained in Wong. Despite the geographical and emotional distance between them, this is what Manhattan's tenement-filled East Village and San Francisco's crowded, tourist-filled Chinatown share: both are populated by people for whom English is not their native tongue. In such a situation, confusion, miscommunication, and misunderstanding are unavoidable and perhaps even inescapable. Wong's awareness of this unbridgeable chasm plays a key role in his work.

In his frontal depictions of gritty, crumbling East Village tenements, which nearly fill the painting's entire surface, and are often framed by a smoldering red sky, Wong suggests that the world is an inferno spiraling toward chaos as well as the decrepit backdrop of his subjects' lives. He underscores this view by placing his figures in the foreground, dwarfed by the moldering tenements and abandoned buildings behind them. By envisioning his urban environment as a stage set, the artist conveys the possibility that its inhabitants are always playing roles, and that everyone is wearing one sort of mask or another in order to survive.

At the same time, Wong suggests that the viewer is an anonymous member of the audience, both a witness and a voyeur. His nighttime paintings, such as *Stanton Near Forsyth Street* (1983), share something with Georges Seurat's moody, nocturnal painting *Circus Sideshow* (1887–88), which is in the collection of the

Metropolitan Museum of Art, New York, where Wong might have seen it. In *Circus Sideshow,* Seurat depicts a group of musicians standing on a stage playing to a crowd of men below, enticing them to buy tickets to see the show.

Seurat depicts the potential ticket buyers in the foreground of the painting, their silhouettes rising from the bottom edge, with their backs to the viewer, suggesting that the viewer is also an anonymous member of the crowd. In *Stanton Near Forsyth Street,* the two figures in the foreground, each standing on opposite sides of the canvas, are the focus of our attention. The Asian figure, who is facing out at the viewer, is Wong, while the figure on the far right, seen in profile, will eventually walk past him or perhaps strike up a conversation and become a lover or a one-night stand. In the sky above, the artist has traced and named the constellations, as well as overlaid the black ground with lines from a poem rendered in both the manual alphabet and Spanish. Along the top strip of the trompe l'oeil wood frame, Wong has "engraved" an ominous line in English: "Morning at the edge of time it never really mattered."

Instead of being an anonymous member of a crowd, we are invisible voyeurs scrutinizing a potential exchange between two men. By placing us in this position, Wong challenges us to examine our response to a covert situation unfolding in a lovingly rendered, utterly bleak circumstance: Do we wish to look the other way and pretend we don't see what's going on? Do we disapprove? Is it none of our business? Are we members of this community or clueless outsiders?

One of the currents running throughout Wong's work is his awareness of the gulf between the viewer and the viewed, between the "I" and the other. Instead of breaking down the fourth or imaginary wall between the actors on the painting's stage and the audience, Wong emphasized its existence, as he did in the multipanel *Chinese Hand Laundry* (1984) and in paintings such as *The Annunciation According to Mikey Pinero (Cupcake and Paco)* (1984); *Lock-Up* (1985); *Cell Door Slot* (1986); *C76, Junior* (1988); and *Mintaka* (1990).

In each of these paintings, Wong utilized trompe l'oeil Realism to render or frame a scene in which the viewer, who is literally and metaphorically *outside* the drama, becomes a voyeur or mute witness. In *C76, Junior,* Wong depicts a Latino man tucked into his bed, asleep and peaceful. This compassionate image is countered by the position of the viewer, who is standing in the corridor outside a prison cell (which is numbered C76). Are we the guard, a potential threat, a guardian angel, or a desiring lover? In *Reckless* (1991), which can be seen as a counterpoint to *C76, Junior,* the cell doors are open and the bare-chested man lying in his bed, with arms folded seductively across his lower belly just above his crotch, which is covered by a sheet, evokes both homoerotic desire and danger. One of the strongest bodies of work within Wong's diverse oeuvre consists of his collaborations with Miguel Piñero. According to Yasmin Ramirez, the two met in 1982 at the opening of *The Crime Show* at ABC No Rio, a storefront art gallery run by members of an artist's collaborative known as Colab.[6]

In their first collaboration, *Attorney Street: Handball Court with Autobiographical Poem by Piñero* (1982–84), Wong includes English, ASL, and graffiti that had been spray-painted on the playground wall. The impetus for the painting came from Piñero, who asked Wong to "document a handball court that had been freshly tagged with graffiti by Little Ivan."[7]

Along with Little Ivan's graffiti, Wong includes Piñero's poem, which begins: "I was born in a barrel of butcher knives / raised between two 45's / on a Saturday night when the jungle was bright and the hustlers were stalking their prey." At the bottom of the painting, in the foreground and partially covering the bottom edge of a graffiti-covered wall, Wong employs the manual alphabet to spell out a line that Piñero spoke in the movie *Fort Apache: The Bronx* (1981): "It's the real deal Neal I'm going to rock your world make your planets twirl, ain't no wack attack." Wong repeats this line in English in a "stamped" metal plaque he has carefully rendered in paint and "attached" to the "wood" frame.

Each language—from the trompe l'oeil letters "stamped" in metal to the stylized hands of ASL to the signature flourishes of the graffiti—required Wong to employ a different convincing imitation to reflect the different realities. Whether derived from literature, tabloid headlines, or something he heard, poetry and the lingua franca of everyday life were an essential part of Wong's paintings from the beginning. In *La Vida* (1988), which shows the facade of a blocked-up, abandoned tenement, Wong depicted men, women, and children in each of the windows of this inaccessible building, including Piñero, who is depicted three times, and another poet and playwright, Amiri Baraka. By combining image and word, as he did in so many paintings, particularly those incorporating lines from the work of Piñero, Wong connected himself to the classical Chinese tradition in which image and ideogram are inseparable.

The lessons Wong absorbed from Johns, Warhol, van Gogh, Chinese classical art, and trompe l'oeil painters such as John F. Peto, give us a glimpse into the breadth of his self-education as well as the disparate visual strands he was able to pull together and make into his own. Even though Wong treats the world as a stage set, suggesting that everyone is wearing a mask or playing a role, he is neither cynical about his characters nor suspicious of their motives. If anything, he is sympathetic to their doomed trajectory and can often convey a tenderness toward masculine figures that is seldom seen in modern and postmodern art.

The Poet's World

(on Matthew Wong)

IN HIS BRIEF time as an artist, Matthew Wong (1984–2019) addressed a paradox that haunts artists who work in traditional mediums: how do you accommodate the medium while also becoming yourself? It takes some artists years to become themselves, while others seem to balance traditions and individuality from the outset. Wong belongs to the latter group.

For Wong, an artist of Chinese descent, living and working in Hong Kong, Zhongshan, China, and Edmonton, Canada—the East and the West—the paradox encompasses cultural and racial considerations. I think this is reflected in his choice to work with ink, which he continued to use throughout the rest of his life.

In 2012, shortly after Wong graduated from the City University of Hong Kong School of Creative Media with an MFA in photography, he began drawing. In 2014, in an interview in online magazine *Altermodernists*, he stated that he initially started with a sketchbook and a bottle of ink and making "a mess every day randomly."

He also stated:

> Art is all-encompassing in my daily life. When I'm not working, I'm at the library doing research into the history of art, figuring out where I can fit into the greater dialogue between artists throughout time, or on the internet looking at art-related websites and engaging in

> dialogue on social media with artists and art-world figures around the world.

Wong had his debut solo show in New York at Karma in 2018. His second show at Karma, *Matthew Wong: Blue* was posthumous. While it was apparent from his first exhibition that drawing was central to his practice, and that he proceeded mark by mark, it was not clear until his exhibition *Matthew Wong: Footprints in the Wind, Ink Drawings, 2013–2017*, at Cheim & Read (2021) just how deeply his work was rooted in the practice of ink drawing on rice paper.

Rice paper was invented in China at the beginning of the Tang Dynasty (618–907 CE). Initially used to write on, it was not until the Yuan Dynasty (1279–1368) ruled China that artists who wanted to break away from previous generations began painting in ink on rice paper rather than silk. I cannot imagine that Wong did not know this history. It seems that consciously being a Chinese artist was the foundation upon which he began and from which he never wavered, even as he absorbed a wide range of references and influences. In the catalogue published on the occasion of this exhibition, Dawn Chan writes:

> We know that Wong specifically fixed his attention on the art of Shitao, as well as those of his [Shitao's] contemporary, Bada Shanren. Both artists were famous for pushing the envelope in their work—for moving ink painting towards surprising moments of expressive abstraction. Their influence is deeply integrated in Wong's own works. Wong maintained a committed ink-art practice, making an ink painting every morning. Painting immediately after waking, before food or coffee, he experimented boldly with the medium, pouring paint and letting it pool on the page.

It seems to me that this should change how we look at Wong. Instead of seeing him as a self-taught Chinese artist gesturing toward the work of Western artists such as Vincent van Gogh, Lois Dodd, and Julian Schnabel for inspiration and guidance, as both

Roberta Smith and Jerry Saltz proposed, he was absorbing the work of Western artists through the lens of Chinese art, specifically ink painting, which, unlike oil painting, cannot be revised or scraped away, as well as carved lacquerware.

Like the older Chinese artist Liu Xiaodong (b. 1963), who has expanded the common view of Realism and observational painting by working on site, often on a monumental scale, Wong has broadened what is commonly defined as calligraphic art and painting based on mark making. Liu redefined observational painting in order to subvert the propagandistic idealization of Russian-style Socialist Realism, which he learned in school, while Wong expanded ink painting out of a desire to make a space in which the two cultures that shaped him fit together. For these reasons this exhibition is important to an understanding of Wong's work. It charts his development as well as underscores his decisiveness and self-directed drive.

Given the misguided view among many Westerners of Chinese art as a tradition based on copying, it is not surprising that the New York art world has qualified its recognition of Liu and Wong as innovative artists who moved both Western art (Realism) and Chinese art (abstract mark making) in a new direction.

In *Untitled* (Ink on rice paper, 15½" x 27", 2013), the earliest work in the exhibition, Wong stains the absorbent paper with different densities of ink, ranging from deep black to washy gray, essentially eschewing the calligraphic line. It is, of course, calligraphy that most appealed to Western artists interested in line, from van Gogh to Mark Tobey and Robert Motherwell.

By staining the paper with irrevocable shapes and marks, Wong undercut any evidence of tentativeness that he might have felt. What is remarkable about this early ink is the degree of conviction with which Wong evokes a complex, atmospheric space of near and far.

Wong's process for the ink drawings was incremental. In *Untitled* (Ink on paper, 31" x 57½", 2014), he pours ink as well as uses a loaded and a dry brush, depending on what he is after. As with the 2013 work, the subject is an abstract landscape that viewers cannot quite identify. Each mark, series of marks, or shape, seems to have called him to make another in response.

In *Untitled* (Ink on paper, 30 $\frac{3}{4}$" x 57 $\frac{1}{4}$", 2014), the dense, irregular grid of ragged, crisscrossing bands is made entirely by pouring, with the bands spreading in different areas and intervals. Already, in these early works, which are large in scale, the viewer should get a strong sense of Wong's restlessness and openness; he was neither looking for a signature style, nor trying to find a formula he could repeat.

By 2015, he was combining large poured areas with swarms of small, repetitive marks, as in the overtly figurative *Untitled* (Ink on paper, 26$\frac{3}{4}$" x 22$\frac{1}{8}$"), which is dominated by a silhouette of what looks like a young girl that stretches from the paper's top to bottom edge, amid a welter of vertical and horizontal marks of varying lengths and widths. A large, triangular opening in the silhouette's rounded face is filled with lines, bonding her to the surroundings. The opening is echoed by another triangle that defines the space separating the nape of her neck, a braid of hair, and her shoulder. A thick brushstroke curving gently down from the front of the girl's neck to the drawing's bottom edge accentuates her connection with the surroundings, as the space between the brushstroke and her chest is filled with lines that are similar to those outside the line.

The year 2015 also marks the first time Wong titled a work. In the vertical *A Poet's World,* the silhouette of an outlined head and solidly stained body encounter a largely black, abstract landscape in the foreground. The dark landscape at the bottom edge transitions in the middle to outlined leaves and a pattern of parallel lines set at different angles. Above and beyond the figure and foreground, Wong has made a series of vertical lines, with a variety of marks in between. In the upper part of a tree trunk near the left edge, he has written the work's title in ideograms. It is a world both real and imagined—which is the paradox at the heart of Wong's work.

It seems to me that Wong strongly identified with the Southern School of Chinese painters working in ink wash. Also known as the literati painters, they were more interested in inner realities than the outward appearances and devotion to realistic detail favored by artists associated with the Northern School. It is best to look at Wong's art from this perspective.

Remarkable as this might seem, it strikes me that by 2015—just three years after he first devoted himself to art and drawing in ink—he had found his subject and assembled an abstract vocabulary of pouring, staining, and linework to create an entire world that is parallel to ours.

One of the recurring subjects of the literati painters was a lone traveler observing nature. This became a motif in Wong's concentrated views of the inside of a flower or a figure gazing at the stars. At times, as in *Winter Wind* (2016), the hooded figure exudes a melancholia that brings to mind the work of Edvard Munch.

In *Odyssey* (2017), an ascending path recedes into the distance, curving behind a dense archway of black tree trunks. Home is something you imagine and long for, but which you neither reach nor see come into view.

David Diao Contemplates an Unwelcoming Chair

IN HONOR OF David Diao's art practice, I thought I should check the databases of four New York museums to see if any had his work in their collection. After all, he is in his late seventies, has been exhibiting in New York since 1969, and was included in the 1973 and 2014 Whitney Biennials. I learned that Diao had one painting dating from 1969 in the Whitney Museum of American Art and none in the Museum of Modern Art, Guggenheim Museum, or Metropolitan Museum of Modern Art. It seems that the institutions that house many of the works and artists he has responded to have not embraced his ongoing critique of Western abstraction's multiple legacies.

Diao's invisibility reminded me that, shortly after I moved to New York in 1975 and well into the late 1980s, I would often be called "David" when I was in Soho looking at art. Once, the dealer Leo Castelli walked past me on West Broadway and said, "Hello, David," in that formal way he had. Even people who knew me would have lapses and call me "David" and then look sheepishly away and hurry on. Concerned as I was about finding my own identity, I wonder if those incidents made me reluctant to write about Diao's work for a long time.

Critics who have championed Diao's career, which began with his first solo show at Paula Cooper in 1969, tend to emphasize that his trajectory can neither be characterized nor encapsulated, at least in terms of style or subject matter. While this is true, such thinking fails to address that Diao has been investigating painting's identities since the outset of his career, often with a critique of the prevailing orthodoxy (i.e., Clement Greenberg and Donald Judd in the late 1960s and '70s) as an integral component. Diao's interest in the identity of the thing he investigates and his resistance to the imperialist attitudes that characterize American midcentury art criticism testify to his recognition that he is an outsider by virtue of being born in Chengdu, China, in 1943, and emigrating from Hong Kong to the United States in 1955 to live with his father. His mother and two younger siblings were unable to leave China. Sometimes this sense of being an outsider was overt in his art; other times it was subtle.

Diao combines a unique set of traits among artists engaged with geometric abstraction; he is conceptual, doubtful, funny, autobiographical, racially conscious, terse, biting, coldly satirical, interested in sensuous yet matter-of-fact surfaces, willing to expose his process, contradictory, and resistant to developing a signature style as an aesthetic commodity. I believe the reasons for this resistance are inextricable from his awareness that he would always be regarded as a non-native.

In a 1963 interview with Gene Swenson, Andy Warhol said: "Somebody said my life has dominated me. [. . .] I liked that idea." This is how Hal Foster understood Warhol's remark in *Pop* (2005): "If you can't beat it, join it; more, if you enter it totally, you might expose it; you might reveal its enforced automatism through your own excessive example." Foster's observation works if you are a white male artist (even a queer one), but you cannot join something that won't have you.

The art world has never quite known what to do with Diao's exposures, and—as he knows and has addressed with deadpan wit—his career is one that has bumped repeatedly into a glass ceiling. He is a conceptual painter whose interest in dates and history, among much else, defines a territory that borders that of the decade-older artist On Kawara (1932–2014) and the nearly two-decade younger Byron Kim (b. 1961). It seems to me that Diao has been the least understood of this group of notional painters. This might be partially because he has pursued many separate and overlapping strands related to history, race, biography, pop culture, language, art history and its exclusionary beliefs, just to name the most obvious.

In his exhibition *David Diao: Berlin Chair in Pieces* at Postmasters Gallery (2022), which has represented him for many years, Diao's ostensible subject is the Berlin chair (1923) designed by Gerrit Rietveld and built and painted by Gerard A. van de Groenekan. The Berlin chair, made of eight solid oak panels cut to a specific size with each board lacquered in black, gray, or white, is the first asymmetrical piece of furniture that Rietveld designed. A copy of the chair is suspended from the gallery ceiling.

The first work that I encountered in this exhibition of thirteen paintings was *Rietveld's Berlin Chair parts on red, yellow, blue* (2021). Against a ground divided into three equal areas of red, yellow, and blue, Diao has overlaid the eight separate parts, each painted monochromatically in black, gray, and white, and aligned vertically like columns in a chart. What comes across first is the pleasure of the painting. Its surface is a tight, palpable skin of acrylic that has been laid down in layers by a palette knife. This combination of tactility, sensuality, and the non-gestural is also present in Rietveld's chairs, as well as Barnett Newman's collectively titled series of large paintings *Who's Afraid of Red, Yellow and Blue*, in which he worked asymmetrically for the first time, and paintings made by Brice Marden in the 1970s that referred to Newman. In fact, one of the many pleasures of *Rietveld's Berlin Chair parts on red, yellow, blue* is its combination of European and American sources, suggesting they are not as separate as many critics announcing the triumph of American art have asserted.

One key to understanding Diao's art is that he has long worked with a reductive geometric vocabulary, while always pushing back against any of postmodernism's reductive narratives, denying subjectivity. Diao is engaged with what Marcel Duchamp called the retinal, even as he is committed to embracing the intellectual and "[putting] painting once again at the service of the mind." This is how Duchamp put it in an interview with James Johnson Sweeney:

> There was no thought of anything beyond the physical side of painting. No notion of freedom was taught. No philosophical outlook was introduced.

What finally distinguishes Diao from other Conceptual artists—including those, like Peter Halley, who paint—is that he never claimed to be either literal or purely objective. Like an ill-behaved guest, he muddied the situation wherever he went, particularly by repeatedly implicating himself in his art, which contradicts as well as critiques Conceptual Art's claim to objectivity.

The beauty of this exhibition was how much Diao did and evoked, using a limited vocabulary of eight predefined, rectangular, black, gray, and white shapes arranged against abstract grounds that go from monochrome to checkerboard. In *Rietveld's Berlin Chair parts forming a circle, Green* (2021), his placement of the varied rectangles invites viewers to see the circumference of the circle in their mind's eye. This interplay between the visible and invisible is not a territory associated with geometric abstraction or Conceptual Art, which emphasizes the literal.

In *Rietveld's Berlin Chair parts describing a square-magenta* (2021), he goes a step further by arranging the eight bands in four kitty-corner pairings to describe the edges of a square, prompting our attention to oscillate between the bands and the space they enclose. That inventive playfulness with limited means is one of the things that sets Diao apart from other artists engaging with modernism's utopian, purist legacy, particularly since he does not anchor his works to a supporting counter or critical narrative. The other compelling thing about these paintings is the seamless merging of sensual surfaces with rich color, such as magenta. After Diao is satisfied with the ground, he draws in pencil where the bands will go and then fills in the color, using a palette knife to apply paint and tape to keep the edges straight. When he peels off the tape, one can still see the pencil lines, bringing to mind Harold Rosenberg's description of an "Action Painting": "What was to go on the canvas was not a picture but an event."

This, I think, is Diao's real achievement. For all their seeming simplicity and visual pleasure, there is a lot to unpack in these paintings. Once you start unpacking them, you never know where you might end up. Take Reitveld's unassembled, uncomfortable, asymmetrical chair, for example. Did Diao pick it only because of its geometric vocabulary? Or was it also, as I began to think, a sign that the art world's institutions have never invited him inside and offered him a seat at the table?

VII.

Capitalist Utopias

(on Tammy Nguyen)

I HAVE NEVER ASKED Tammy Nguyen if she knows of this statement by Stéphane Mallarmé, "Everything in the world exists in order to end up as a book," although it makes sense that she would. In 2017, after meeting her at an Asian American Literature Festival hosted by the Smithsonian Asian Pacific American Center in Washington, D.C., I thought of her as a book artist and subscribed to Passenger Pigeon Press, which she started in 2016. What I have since learned is that she has a very elastic vision of what constitutes a book.

Nguyen has designed and printed offset editions, made letterpress books that include laser-cut technology, dense collages, prints, and large paintings on paper that has been stretched around a wood panel and displayed on the wall. Marbling, chine collé, gold and silver leafing, and calligraphic brushwork are some of the processes that she utilizes in her work. She has studied different disciplines, including the taxidermy of birds, when she worked at the Yale Peabody Museum of Natural History while earning her MFA, and lacquer painting when she was in Vietnam on a Fulbright (2007–8).

In her paintings, which arise out of firsthand experience, buttressed by historical and scientific research, she combines aspects of illuminated manuscripts, manga, watercolor, and calligraphic gestures to address specific geographic situations in Southeast

Asia in a time of global expansion, as well as territorial disputes over shipping lanes, capitalist investment, utopian fantasies about gated communities, climate change, and her own family history.

One of three exhibitions on the theme of water curated by Rachel Vera Steinberg, *Tammy Nguyen, Freehold* at Smack Mellon (2021) brought together the work stemming from her latest investigation into Southeast Asia, specifically—as the press release states—"Forest City, a tax free, man-made island in Johor, Malaysia, located along the Singapore Strait and adjacent to the Strait of Malacca—one of the busiest trade conduits in the world."

Advertising itself as "a smart and green futuristic city," Forest City will "create an ideal, idyllic and technology-driven living and working space ecosystem." It sounds perfect, doesn't it? Who wouldn't want to live there, at least part of the year? Posing as a potential investor, Nguyen went to the island to look at the real estate and amenities, which included a gym, a spa, fine dining, and a golf course, all the activities you might expect of a postmodern full-service paradise.

There has always been something both methodical and thorough about the way Nguyen approaches a subject. For this exhibition, she designed and made a flag and flagpole, which is in the exhibition, along with a photograph of it in a field in Connecticut. What's a man-made utopian island without a flag? Nguyen's flag is composed of a white circle (a sacred sun in the center of a field of twelve alternating green-and-blue stripes, signifying land and water, all existing in perfect harmony.

There is something wry and even melancholy about planting the flag of a real estate fantasy in the Singapore Strait in a nondescript field in Connecticut. It is the humor of feeling displaced and wondering if there is any place that you belong. Maybe a sense of belonging is a thing of the past, a sign of privilege. This sense of displacement is emphasized by the inclusion of the photograph in the exhibition, and the actual flag with a metal bird of prey topping the flagpole just in front of it.

Three other bodies of work are in the exhibition: two groups of either three or four thematically related paintings and a group of twelve intaglio prints with chine collé and collage, whose titles are taken from the improbable names of container ships—*Treasure, Evergovern, Everglobe,* and *Destiny* are some examples.

In each collage, Nguyen includes the name of the ship, a number referring to the time of day (which doubles as a reminder of the constant role shipping plays in the world's economy), a negative space shaped like a bird of prey, in which another space is glimpsed, images taken from *The 'Nam,* a Marvel comic book series about the Vietnam War that was published from 1986 until '93, and ran for eighty-four issues, and Forest City's striped flag with the sun literally cut out.

By crisscrossing the figure-ground relationship, Nguyen subverts any sense of stability and the comfort that comes with knowing where everything should go. In *Treasure,* we see an aerial view of a landscape within the bird's contours. A bomber is flying in the blue sky framed by one of the bird's wings. Elsewhere, faces are contorted in pain and eyes peer through abstract foliage and holes in the flag. While everything is in a state of disturbance and dislocation, the presentation of the images is cool, the edges carefully delineated. The resulting tension is one of the subjects of the work.

The ironically titled series *Seasons of Revolution* (all dated 2021 and measuring 48" x 36"), consists of four paintings on paper stretched over panel. Each painting depicts different types of tropical foliage, an animal, and a white abstract shape, which evokes Nguyen's symbol of the sacred sun. In these pieces, Nguyen lays down an abstract ground by staining the paper with different hues, whose shapes and tones are used as initial guides to help determine what she will add next. As in much of her work, she complicates the figure-ground relationship.

In their layered, all-over compositions, the *Seasons of Revolution* paintings approach abstraction, but Nguyen deliberately does not cross over. The juxtapositions are not arbitrary. The golf clubs peering through leaves and black bats hanging upside down in

Seasons of Revolution 2 evoke the meeting of manicured landscape and dense foliage at the golf course in Forest City. In addition to their roles in vampire tales, bats have assumed other sinister implications since the World Health Organization connected them with the spread of COVID-19.

In *Seasons of Revolution 1,* crustaceans underscore the rising seas as well as suggest the folly of building a man-made island. Climate change is everywhere, even if, as the press release tells us:

> Her guide informed her that there was "no climate change here." Malaysia, he explained, does not suffer from natural disasters like its neighboring countries.

The exhibition's three largest works focused on an archetype inspired by Nguyen's experience in Forest City and all the different associations and memories her visit stirred up. In *Ape* (2021), she depicts the animal looking back at the viewer, at once bewildered and perplexed; a bird is behind the ape and snakes rise up from below. The work references the movie creature King Kong (there are movie studios in Forest City). For trivia experts who see a reflection of culture in little-remembered facts, it is worth recalling that in *Kong: Skull Island* (2017), the eleventh King Kong film since the first one in 1933, the character of San Lin, the Asian woman biologist, was continually rewritten and reduced until Alison de Souza, in her review in the Singapore newspaper *Straits Times,* described the role as a *hua ping,* meaning a vase, something insignificant in the background, and the actress "hardly does or says a thing."

In the painting *Woman* (2021), it becomes more evident that, as with the ape's fur, only someone who knows calligraphy, the repetition of a set of abstract marks, could have done the different kinds of mark making visible in a terrycloth towel. This is something that viewers ought to recognize—this and other paintings in the exhibition have their roots in the history of Asian art, from Nguyen's use of paper to her mark making. In the towel a set of delicate abstract marks are repeated without becoming rote or predictable.

The woman in the painting comes across as absurd and hilarious. She has cucumber slices covering her eyes (a common beauty treatment) and stands in dense growth. Snakes are entwined in her hair (recalling Medusa), and a speckled, metal leaf bird partially covers her face (is it also a mud pack?) as well as peeks out from behind it. If she is getting a beauty treatment, why is she standing in a tropical landscape, with snakes on both sides of her? The fact that Nguyen's figure seamlessly compresses different narratives and archetypes, from Medusa to a smooth-skinned woman undergoing a spa treatment, is one of the strengths of her artwork. Her paintings and collages are immediate and visually compelling, but still require unpacking. It is with prolonged looking and reflection that Nguyen's intentions begin to reveal themselves.

Chie Fueki Reimagines Portraiture

CHIE FUEKI BELONGS to a very small group of American artists whose work is informed by three radically different cultures: Japan, Brazil, and the United States. This is because she was born in Yokohama, Japan, was raised in São Paulo, Brazil, and immigrated to the US, where she earned her BFA at the Ringling College of Art & Design in Sarasota, Florida, and her MFA at Yale University. Without knowing much else about her, it seems to me that she has lived in four distinct locales and is able to speak three languages. The reason I mention Fueki's background is that, since her solo first exhibition in 2002, she has been quietly creating a singular body of mind-bending work that has never fit into the New York art world, which is governed by a whole host of unspoken conventions, such as the legacy of Minimalism and the distrust of craft and ornament.

One of fifteen inaugural recipients of a Joan Mitchell Fellowship (2021), Fueki posted this statement on her website:

> My painting practice is centered around the depiction of figures, symbols, and abstract spaces using multi-layered ornamental surfaces and fields of color. I blend visual languages and culturally coded images drawn from my experience growing up in a traditionally-oriented Japanese community in São Paolo, Brazil.

For her debut solo exhibition, *Chie Fueki: You and I*, at DC Moore Gallery, the artist showed five large portraits done in acrylic and mixed media on mulberry paper mounted on wood. Collage, paint, and appliqué are just some of the materials and processes Fueki employs. The result is multilayered work that—despite everything she puts into it—still feels airy and open.

In the press release she described her work further:

> I consider myself a mixed-language painter with interest in eastern and western perspectival systems, architectural graphics, pop animation, pre-Renaissance European painting and exuberant color.

It is clear that Fueki's art pushes against the constraints of Western painting, beginning with her process of working on paper, which she mounts on wood, as well as her use of different culturally coded images and perspectival systems. In this regard she shares something with two other Asian American artists who work on paper in innovative ways, Jiha Moon and Tammy Nguyen. Fueki's use of paper, paint, and collage culminates in both a compressed surface and a complex spatiality, in which the ornamental and nonrealistic color play a significant role. With its radiating lines, patterns, and evocations of force fields, often done in what she calls "exuberant color," the effects are ravishing and mystifying.

One of the first things I noticed about these portraits is that the only face that is visible is one reflected in a mirror in *finally Bridget* (2021), which depicts a friend of the artist after they have transitioned. The fact that we see only the subject's reflection conveys something about Fueki's approach: it is always indirect or from an unexpected angle, as in *Kyle (High Fidelity)* (2021), whose subject we see from behind, seated and wearing headphones. Fueki works in what I would call a state of imaginative recollection, with a heightened sense of reality. She is equally attentive to the environment in which her subject or subjects are located, as she does not seem to believe that a portrait is limited to one's appearance, which is the hallmark of Western portrait painting.

The subject of *Catherine* (2021) is the painter Catherine Murphy, who was Fueki's teacher at Yale, and has since become a friend. As someone who has written about Murphy many times over the years, including her most recent show, and who wrote the first monograph on her work, I was doubly delighted by this painting. Fueki is able to create a number of symbols and images inspired by Murphy's work without making viewers feel like they need to know the source.

We see a cropped view of Murphy in profile; her head is a blue semicircle extending in from the right edge, while her arm is made of four different-sized, gray geometric shapes, one of which seems to have been bitten into, leaving a large, jagged opening on the bottom edge of her forearm. While these shapes can be seen as a nod to Murphy's interest in geometry, they also function as solid forms that are part of the composition's mixture of patterns, lines, and marks. Fueki's use of lines and dots imbues the paintings with varying states of heightened opticality.

The artist is holding a brush and painting the left edge of the canvas, as if it were a flat surface. Above the hand we see the name CATHY backward, a nod to Murphy's painting *Cathy* (2001), in which she "wrote" her name backward on the outside of a steamed-up window in winter. At the same time, the backward name calls the logic of the picture plane into question, as the name seems to be floating, suggesting that the layered space of this work is not purely material. This feeling of an ambiguous spatiality is underscored by the radiating lines contained within saw-toothed forms set in different parts of the composition. Are they signs of force fields and visible representations of an otherwise unseen world?

Fueki makes paintings that invite us to look slowly. They are layered with images ranging from the figural to the abstract (i.e., geometric patterns and shapes) to marks (dots and lines). In *Brides (Hilary and Ara)* (2021), the ground changes from porous red in the upper half to an enigmatic surface below. By making the pictorial space ambiguous, the distinct, detailed forms she affixes to the surface seem to float. Along with her innovative combinations of collage and appliqué, another distinguishing feature of the work is her interruption of diaphanous fields of color with distinct shapes in different colors whose surfaces are defined by ornamental and allusive curlicues, suggestive of lace embroidery. And if this were not enough to take in, what are we to make of the black cat scampering across the lower third of the painting or the butterflies seen throughout?

In Fueki's world, the solid and ephemeral can seem indistinguishable from each other. Near the top of *Brides (Hilary and Ara)* are two outlined circles just below a solid red circle with a darker red heart at its center. Red lines radiate from the sunlike orb. Do they represent the sun's rays or the presence of divine light? What about the heart? While Fueki's composition seems to have been inspired by *The Arnolfini Wedding* (1434) by Jan van Eyck, she has also methodically replaced all of the former's symbols with her own, starting with the cat taking the place of the early breed of Griffon Bruxellois seen at the couple's feet in the van Eyck. This fastidiousness is characteristic of Fueki's approach. No matter how busy or densely layered her painting, nothing feels extraneous or unconsidered. In a time of fabrication and outsourcing, her hands-on approach might seem old fashioned, but you would be wrong to think so. The pleasure of making rings true in all of her work. At once radical, generous, and self-effacing, Fueki's collapsing together of work and pleasure challenges the mainstream's preoccupation with sybaritic leisure and the selfies that record it.

Jiha Moon's Breakthrough

I FIRST MET JIHA Moon in 2000, when she was in the MFA program at the University of Iowa. Later, I learned that she was born in Daegu, South Korea, in 1973, and came to the United States in the late 1990s after getting her BFA and MFA in Korea. At that point, she was working largely in painting and printmaking. In 2012, she was awarded a grant from the Museum of Contemporary Art of Georgia, which she used to sign up at a local clay studio in Atlanta, where she has lived for many years.

The reason I mention these facts about Moon's life is that in her exhibition of paintings and ceramics *Jiha Moon: Stranger Yellow* (2022) at Derek Eller Gallery, she joined together images and symbols from the different cultures where she has lived, from her upbringing in a city known for its textiles (Daegu) to her many years as a resident of the only city to be set on fire during the Civil War, the birthplace of Martin Luther King Jr. and the Civil Rights Movement, and the city where a man, targeting Asian women, shot six to death during another wave of anti-Asian hate crimes in 2021.

In nearly every work, the color yellow—as stylized brushstroke, sinuous wave, or banana peel—plays a role. While some might see Moon's work as a hybrid of East and West, I have come to agree with the great Antillean writer Edouard Glissant that "hybrid" conveys predictability. Glissant's term "creolization," which underscores the continuous flux and absorption of different cultures and locales, more accurately characterizes Moon's bricoleur approach to living in the diaspora. That's because I always encounter something unpredictable in her art, as she must in her life. And it is precisely her openness to using any source—from classic Asian symbols to kitsch fantasy to Pop Art to mall culture to Korean and American folk art—that makes her work flamboyant, captivating, odd, funny, smart, uncanny, comically monstrous, unsettling, and, most of all, over-the-top.

There were times at the exhibition when I did not know how I was supposed to feel while looking at one of Moon's works. They achieve a deliciously vertiginous state of ambivalence by bringing together a wide variety of diverse cultural sources, which, contrary to what one might expect, does not flatten them out. Moon has clearly pushed her work into fresh territory, and in her ceramics and paintings she is making that territory her own. Her art does not resemble anyone else's, and for that alone she should be getting far more attention than she has.

The painting *Yellowave (Stranger Yellow)* (2021) is a diptych done in ink and acrylic on hanji, a traditional handmade Korean paper that dates back to the first century BCE, mounted on canvas. Moon's materials remind viewers that her roots are not in Western painting, even as it has had an impact on her thinking and processes.

Using a palette dominated by yellow with touches of turquoise, blue, and brown, she depicts ribbonlike waves extending in from both sides toward the center. Overlapping as well as running parallel to each other, the layered waves partially cover four small rectangles, two in each panel. In one of the panels is the silhouette of a turtle, as if seen from above, while the others convey different levels of legibility.

The strength of *Yellowave (Stranger Yellow)* lies in the ambiguity of the waves. Are they stylized brushstrokes, blond tresses, or animated gusts of wind blowing across a landscape where we can glimpse fences, a symbol of two birds kissing, and the silhouettes of fortune cookies and turtles? Moon has moved away from her earlier, more literal reference (Roy Lichtenstein's graphic image of a brushstroke) by dislodging the amplified mark from any one-to-one reading. Starting out as a quotation, Lichtenstein's brushstroke has slowly morphed into another resonant sign in Moon's vocabulary. Instead of citing it, as she once did, she has absorbed a stylized yellow brushstroke into her lexicon, just as Lichtenstein consumed and transformed a loaded, drippy Abstract Expressionist brushstroke into one of his signature images.

In the painting *Yellowave (Blue)* (2021), using a palette of deep blues, faded reds, bright banana yellows, and midnight blacks, Moon depicts a blue-and-yellow streaked wave-brushstroke winding (or unwinding) within the square format. The wave-brushstroke transforms into a creature that seems equal parts phoenix, dragon, snake, and squid. Her evocation of a state of continuous change has roots in both Jackson Pollock's drip paintings and the depictions of mythic dragons and phoenixes, which are mortal enemies, found throughout Asian art. This is where she has taken the brushstroke that was originally inspired by Lichtenstein.

This is the breakthrough that Moon has made in her paintings: they are an amalgamation of Eastern and Western sources that cannot be easily taken apart. The joining of the two has become seamless. Something fresh is being made. If the exhibition consisted only of the three paintings, it would still amount to a remarkable accomplishment that addresses the construction of an unpredictable identity by someone living in the diaspora. The fact that it also contains more than twenty ceramic works elevates this show to another level. The simplest way to characterize Moon's ceramics is to state that she has merged the vessel with a creature. Sometimes the creature has a head, torso, and feet. Other times it is just a head, signified by a large garish mouth full of menacing teeth—a combination of the comic and grotesque.

In her ceramics, Moon has synthesized face jugs, teapots, and incense burners. She glazes and paints the entire surface, both inside and outside, and attaches various objects, including ceramic fortune cookies, banana peels, pinkish round forms topped by red nipples, and synthetic hair. I think of her ceramics as household gods, mythic creatures, animal spirits, dolls, and idols, whose exact motivations remain elusive. Are they benign or sinister presences? Do they protect us? Or are they tricksters?

What connects this diverse body of work is Moon's penchant for painting images and patterns on the surface, as well as adding on different representational objects. The result is a complex figural presence that resists any quick reading. One sign of her increasing deftness is her repeated use of ceramic fortune cookies, which retain their recognizable shape but become different in each work, depending on how she paints their surface and where they are placed. They can be eyes, ears, hats, or handles. Meanwhile, the images she depicts run the gamut, from *milagros* to Asian Pop culture, from cosmic signs to comic symbols. Moon's creatures inhabit a world on the verge of going amok.

By layering and colliding images from different cultures and beliefs, and by adding unwieldy things to the surface, Moon underscores how difficult it is for an Asian woman to navigate American culture in order to make a room of one's own, to quote Virginia Woolf. Moon made a room of her own with this exhibition; it was a layered space expanding beyond the singular to a greater and more nuanced understanding of identity. The things attached to bodies could be emotional baggage, things that stick to the individual, deservedly or not, or what one takes along when uprooted. In contrast to Woolf's quiet sanctuary, the only room a Korean woman living in the diaspora has is the one that she carries wherever she goes. Moon's ceramic figures are both a sign of stability and something to be protected and carried when it becomes necessary to leave your home.

In Praise of Illegibility

(on Nadia Haji Omar)

THERE IS A strain of abstract art that I don't remember ever being the subject of an exhibition in New York, a city where more than six hundred languages are spoken and written: asemic writing. An exhibition focusing on "writing without the smallest unit of meaning" could include works by Xu Bing, Henri Michaux, J. B. Murry, Cy Twombly, and Isidore Isou, founder of Lettrism. To this distinguished company, which transcends cultural boundaries, I would add Nadia Haji Omar, whose work I first wrote about in 2018.

Haji Omar, who was born in Melbourne, Australia, and raised in Sri Lanka, grew up learning different languages (Arabic, Sinhalese, Tamil, English, and French), some of which she studied after moving to the United States. It is out of the confluence of Western, Asian and South Asian cultures—she is of Syrian, Indian, and Sri Lankan descent—and their written languages that she has developed a visual vocabulary of lines and dots.

Her exhibition *Nadia Haji Omar: Secret Garden*, at Kristen Lorello (2022), included twenty-six works on paper done between 2017 and 2022. Given the amount of letters in the English alphabet, I don't think the number of works was arbitrary. It is also worth noting that the Sinhala alphabet has sixty letters, of which only fifty-seven are needed, while the Tamil alphabet has two hundred and forty-seven letters.

Working in graphite, colored pencil, acrylic, ink, watercolor, dye, and wax, Haji Omar makes intimately scaled drawings (between 8" x 6" and 12" x 9") in which she repeats small abstract marks and shapes, along with flowers and eyes. Although a few of the titles suggest these are studies for paintings, all the drawings stand on their own. Despite her circumscribed vocabulary, in which repetition plays a strong role, Haji Omar does not settle for making variations on a theme—each work is distinct.

In the ink and graphite drawing *December* (2017), the artist uses six different configurations (according to my calculation) of dots and lines to make an asymmetrical abstract composition. They include two stacks of loose linear bands containing wayward rows of stacked rectangles, each filled with a dot alternating with rows of blank space, oddly rounded outlined shapes that bring to mind jigsaw puzzles and aerial maps of lakes, a thin band whose interior is marked by a row of single dots, and other simple and precise configurations.

The first drawing I saw when I entered the Kristen Lorello gallery was *Square Font* (2020), composed of a checkerboard pattern of tiny black-and-white squares. In each white square is a red dot. Within this field are script-like rows of red squares with black dots and black squares with red dots. Each row brings to mind computer pixels and the relationship between letters, signs, and grids.

While *Square Font* evokes digital signs, the time-consuming process of making the drawing raises questions about time-saving devices. What do we gain and what do we lose with each new invention? The fact that the shapes never become letters and the rows do not become sentences is part of the work's meaning. Can we look for the sake of looking, or must looking always be about gaining and extraction?

In their invitation to be read, and their successful resistance to legibility, Haji Omar's asemic works open up a space that is their own. I don't think she is making a secret language or script, which is what the visionary black artist J. B. Murry believed he was creating at the behest of a higher being. The tension between what is almost readable and completely unreadable speaks to us on many levels, starting with our desire to know what we are looking at and why. In *Dark Eyes (the flower)* (2020), the artist's use of pink and red—and her floral motif—inflect her calligraphic, script-like lines, but do not make apparent what they might mean.

In *Study for Dear So and So Painting* (2018), Haji Omar stops within a hair's breadth of being decipherable. The awkwardness of the script brought to mind rows of unreadable handwriting. I was reminded of letters that never get sent or received, the dilemma of wanting to say something but feeling that you don't have exactly the right words for it. For me, the drawing stirred up the frustration of feeling inarticulate that afflicts us all when it comes to communication. Our inability to exchange ideas and adequately transmit our thoughts has been exacerbated by the extreme isolation people experienced during the COVID-19 lockdown.

In a country where anti-Muslim sentiment runs strong, Haji Omar's use of an unreadable calligraphic script can be read a number of ways. For one, it touches on this country's cynical psyche as well as its promotion of a monolingual society. The drawings obliquely address this and other loaded subjects. Hers is an art of concentrated attention, a record of small acts of devotion, and of counting time as well as shaping one's passage through it. It is about the beauty that can be obtained with simple, widely available materials, and on a small scale. In that alone, Haji Omar is critiquing how we spend our time and our materialist desires.

An Understated, Auspicious Debut

(on Hannah Lee)

Being bowled over by an unknown artist's first one-person show does not happen often, but when it does, it renews your faith that the art world is not just about buzz and hype. That is how I felt when I saw the work in *Hannah Lee: First Language* at Entrance (2021-2022). The gallery's press release, less than half a page long and jargon-free, with the artist's three-sentence biography located at the bottom, was refreshing to read. After receiving a BFA at Parsons School of Design in 2012, Lee did not go on to earn an MFA at Yale or Columbia or any other graduate program. This was a press release in which no claims were being made for Lee's pedigree, which meant that the work would have to speak for itself. I can count the number of times this has happened in the past few years on one hand, especially for an artist's debut show.

Lee exhibited six modestly scaled paintings and group of small sculptural objects composed of Q-tips propped up in melting ice cubes made of resin, sitting on two narrow glass shelves. The paintings (all dated 2020 or 2021) were done in oil or oil and wax on panel. The largest measures 30 x 40 inches, and the smallest 8 x 8 inches.

No matter how straightforward some of Lee's realist scenes seem to be, their clarity tilts toward the dreamlike rather than the observed or remembered. Pressed to characterize her work, I would call it "liminal realism." She depicts an uncanny situation so that it may initially strike the viewer as believable, which might be considered the opposite of Surrealism. Lee's work quickly and smoothly draws the viewer into its clearly defined space, yet resists immediate comprehension. I liked being in that ambiguous state, where seeing and knowing dance around each other without letting go.

In *Milk* (2020), two fit, young Asian women, seated cross-legged on blue satin mats placed on a wooden floor, face each other from the opposite ends of a long, low, narrow blue table, which is inlaid with a scene of pairs of horses and swans made of abalone shells. At the far end, one of the women, who is bare breasted and wears black sweatpants, is pressing a pump to each breast. Near the other end of the table, the pumps' tubes carry milk into a glass. Although her back is to us, the woman sitting in front of the glass appears younger and slightly smaller in stature than her companion.

The age difference suggests they are sisters rather than mother and daughter. I suppose they could be friends, but that relationship seems unlikely to me. There are many ways to read this sibling relationship, the coolness of the older woman's face and the unseen face of the younger woman, and yet none strikes me as fully satisfying, which is why I feel so strongly about this painting. It does not fit into any tropes regarding familial relationships, particularly those in an Asian American family, which have become commonplace in middlebrow magazines and articles about "tiger moms" and model immigrant behavior.

The other thing that struck me about the paintings is that their locales and figures are all different from each other. Lee does not step into the same subject twice. In *In Between* (2021), she focuses on the far wall of a gray, nearly empty room. A door is at each end of the wall, both slightly ajar, their doorknobs mirroring each other. Between the doors, an illuminated fish tank sits on an equally sized table. On the left is an electrical cord that reaches from the fish tank to a socket on the wall. On the right side, two clear plastic tubes extend from inside the fish tank to the slightly open door on the right. There are no fish in the tank, just some rocks and water.

Often, the problem with discordant works like this is that they can feel contrived or arbitrary, but I did not feel this was true of Lee's paintings, which is why I am drawn to them. She has thought through every decision: the electrical socket, the lighting in the room, the color of the walls and ceiling, and the placement of the doorknobs. If anything, the weirdness comes across as natural. For all of Lee's deliberation, there is something direct and offhand about the paintings, something understated.

In *Demonstration* (2020), which was the exhibition's largest painting, I would call attention to the way Lee stages the scene, the care she has paid to the spacing, to architectural details, and to both the two figures facing us. They (a man and a woman) are standing by a column, and those facing away from us compose the audience looking at them. Three of the four people with their backs to us form a diagonal, even as the two on the far left are parallel to the picture plane. Lee's placement of a plant and planter and an electrical wall socket covering on the painting's right-hand side convey her compositional precision. She is gently guiding the direction of our attention. She is encouraging us to become curious about a public demonstration of a product's effectiveness: a woman and a man who seems to be applying eyeliner on her.

What is the purpose of this demonstration? Why is it taking place in this location, which looks like some unused corner of a hotel lobby? Who are the people in the audience? Is this a dream about being singled out for being an Asian woman? Lee seems to be able to strike a perfect balance between transparency and opacity. Rather than impose an external logic on the paintings, which would make them feel artificial, she appears to find it in the process. That's the power of these works.

In *Shower* (2021), which I found to be the most compelling and perplexing painting in the exhibition, Lee depicts a stage-like room within a larger space. The room is cropped on the right side, leaving a view of the front door, with light shining in from the gap between the door and the floor, a single bed in the left corner, gray walls, books and bottles on a board sitting on a radiator, and an open door on the room's far left. Through the door we see a figure standing in a bathtub behind a transparent shower curtain.

Here is where painting seamlessly shifts into another dimension. The wall on this side of the room is just a gray wallboard. We can see a wooden support and brace on the outside, indicating that the room is inside a larger room. And yet, if the wall on the left is all that separates the room from the larger space it is in, how is the person supposed to be standing inside the room taking a shower, when the wall suggests that space cannot exist.

Lee's attention to unlikely details further enhances the mystery of the painting. What is that light glowing in the bed? Is someone reading under the covers? Why is the bed so close to the front door? How big or small is this apartment?

The paucity of creature comforts, such as chairs and other things meant to make one's life comfortable, is a noticeable feature of these works, and yet Lee does not make that the focus of the paintings. Rather, it is something discovered in the looking, just as the pairs of animals seen in the inlay in *Milk* are not immediately obvious. This was one of the strongest debuts I have had the pleasure of experiencing in years. The singular pursuit of the inexplicable that has gone into each painting, along with the artist's disinterest in developing a signature style, conveys an ambition and confidence that speaks well for Lee's future.

VIII.

Martin Puryear and John Keats

RECENTLY, AND RATHER unexpectedly, the term "negative capability," which was coined by the poet John Keats, came to mind. Was this an outlandish association to make while looking at Martin Puryear's exhibition at Matthew Marks? After all, what does the nineteenth-century English Romantic poet Keats, who died at the age of twenty-five, and who published only around fifty not particularly well-received poems in his short lifetime, have to do with a late-twentieth-century Black sculptor in his mid-seventies, who had a highly acclaimed retrospective at the Museum of Modern Art, New York (November 4, 2007–January 14, 2008)? Other than their deep belief in craft and the thing itself (the lyric poem or discrete sculpture), which these days is considered old fashioned, Puryear and Keats seem to have little in common.

And yet, for some not immediately apprehensible reason, while I was looking at a group of nine thematically related sculptures and two prints—all of which were inspired by the pliable red Phrygian cap—I thought back to Keats's belief that the receptivity to experience could enable an artist to transcend historical circumstances. While admittedly the association initially seemed far-fetched, the more I reread Keats and researched the backstory of the red Phrygian cap, the more I realized that there was a deep bond connecting these two disparate figures across time. And, perhaps even more importantly, as I unraveled the connection between these two men, I realized in some concrete way that Puryear had surpassed the achievement of his previous work, while transcending and expanding a variety of contexts in which his work had been seen. It was clear to me that this new development in Puryear's work demanded to be declared and acknowledged—which is to say spelled out.

According to the gallery's press release, the sculptures and prints "were inspired by the form of the felt Phrygian cap, or 'liberty cap' [which] [. . .] was worn as a sign of resistance during the French Revolution and adopted as a symbol of liberty during the American Revolution." It goes on to quote Puryear about the subject, which is depicted on the card by an eighteenth-century print of a Black man wearing a red "liberty cap" with the caption, "*Moi libre aussi*" ("I am free too") beneath him:

> Although I was certainly aware of numerous depictions of this cap in European and early American art when I began work on the *Big Phrygian* sculpture, I only discovered the engraved image of the Black man wearing the red Phrygian cap—the image that appears on the exhibition announcement—years afterwards.

As a symbol used by various individuals and societies to mean freedom and the pursuit of liberty, the red Phrygian cap marks a new kind of source for Puryear. It is both what he did and what he didn't do with the symbol that conveys the nature of the breakthrough he has made in his art.

Big Phrygian (2010–2014) is made of sections of red cedar that have been joined together in a soft, pointed form. The curling upper section is not as tightly sealed as the lower one, with visible seams that prevent the sculpture being read as a single unified form. The visible seams underscore the changes that occur in the form as it curls out while shrinking in space. *Big Phrygian* has been painted with many coats of red veneer, with parts textured like felt. Its form is a sensual and visual paradox, which the artist explores in a variety of different ways in the other related sculptures. Like the soft, felt cap that inspired it, the form diminishes rather swiftly in circumference the farther it gets from the base.

Typically, this means that the spiraling form both extends and withdraws, simultaneously rising, diminishing, and moving outward into the surrounding space; as the top grows smaller, it seems to pull back inside itself, eventually balling into a small, ineffectual fist. With the outward movement of the piece culminating in withdrawal and consolidation, the viewer is invited to contemplate how the tension animating *Big Phrygian* is intrinsic to its meaning.

In the cast ductile iron sculpture *Up and Over* (2014), a curving, seemingly soft form rises up, while leaning forward slightly, until it suddenly flops over, at once clownish and futile. The combination of hard material and soft appearance of *Up and Over* underscores the contradiction that is basic to the form. It can neither overcome its material status nor defy gravity.

In the two-sided sculpture *Faux Vitrine* (2014), which resembles a display case bending over, as if pulled by its own gravitational force, Puryear has made a piece with shelves that changes radically as we walk around it. The polished steel on one side mirrors and breaks up our reflection, while the painted shelves on the other side face away, seemingly unaffected by the mirror-like surfaces. There is neither an ideal vantage point nor any continuity in *Faux Vitrine*. Isn't the viewer's inability to grasp the work in its entirety coupled with its changes part of the meaning of the work?

The visual and physical contradictions arrived at by Puryear, in the three pieces that I have briefly described, posit a complex nexus of possible meanings in the history of sculpture, including a convincing counterpoint to the verticality and aspiration for the spiritual found in the different versions Constantin Brancusi did of his *Endless Column*, beginning with *Version I* (1918), made of carved oak, in the collection of the Museum of Modern Art, New York. Doubt and fruitlessness are bound up in the identity of each of Puryear's *Faux Vitrine*, as are struggle and determination. None of these possibilities, however, supplant the others.

What enhances all of these possibilities is the backstory that Puryear evokes in his allusion to the Phrygian cap, but refuses to nail down. Known for the thoroughness that he brings to bear in all of his work, Puryear makes clear in his statement in the press release that he was engaged with the subject for many years before discovering the engraving. In fact, I want to suggest the possibility that his awareness of the liberty cap dates all the way back to his childhood, growing up in Washington, D.C. It is this possible biographical trace, and the degree to which Puryear has displaced it into his work without having it point back toward him in any obvious way, that further convinced me of his affinity with Keats.

Keats, we might remember, possessed an astonishing ability to contain contending points of view in a single poem, such as in his "La Belle Dame Sans Merci," where sensuality, eros, destruction, and death are embodied in the "Lady without Mercy." At the same time, Keats transcended biography to such a great degree that the "knight," who is "alone and palely loitering" in the opening lines of "La Belle Dame Sans Merci," is both the alter ego of the tubercular Keats and not him at all.

In *Big Phrygian*, Puryear also manages to organize a wide spectrum of contradictions into a single form, something very few artists of any generation are able to accomplish, particularly with such extreme economy. Meanwhile, the sculpture has subsumed any biographical traces, leaving the viewer to conjecture and, more importantly, reflect upon what was experienced and known from history.

I feel confident in saying that Puryear is deeply knowledgeable of the history of the Phrygian cap: from its first instance of signifying freedom and the quest for individual liberty in Europe (it was confused with the Pileus, a brimless, conical felt cap worn by freed Roman slaves) through its incorporation into the coats of arms and flags of many Latin American countries, including Nicaragua, Cuba, and El Salvador. I also cannot help but think that as a symbol of rebellion and self-identification (as it may have occurred to Puryear), the Phrygian cap can be seen as a precursor to the hoodie.

It is while Puryear was growing up in Washington, D.C., that he likely first encountered the symbol of the Phrygian cap. A representation of the cap can be found on the seal of the United States Senate and the Seal of the United States Army. It is on the flag of Haiti and its coat of arms, where it is placed atop a palm tree, signifying the only successful revolution by enslaved people, led by the former slave Toussaint Louverture against their white European owners. While another artist might have chosen to make a sculpture depicting the soft red cap atop a palm tree, giving viewers a literalist work whose meaning is easily accessible and not particularly challenging, Puryear elected to do otherwise. In fact, by choosing to make work in which he could have cited a particular historical context to gain traction for its meaning, yet deliberately not doing so, Puryear equates aesthetic freedom with personal freedom, even as he expresses an unavoidable doubt about whether this idealized state can ever be reached.

Moreover, it is also likely that Puryear was aware that the presence of the Phrygian cap, appearing as it does in well-known signs dotting the nation's capital, is also haunted by its absence: there is a notorious story about its removal from a monument by Thomas Crawford (1814–57) on the order of Jefferson Davis, who was secretary of war at the time, before he went on to become the president of the Confederacy. It seems likely that Crawford, who was married to Julia Ward Howe (1819–1910), the American abolitionist and author of the song "Battle Hymn of the Republic," knew what it could mean to have his monument *Freedom Triumphant in War and Peace* wearing a Phrygian cap, the Roman symbol of an emancipated slave. Davis, a diehard slave owner, who oversaw the project, ordered its removal because "its history renders it inappropriate to a people who were born free and would not be enslaved." *Freedom Triumphant in War and Peace,* which crowns the dome of the US Capitol in Washington, D.C., is wearing a military helmet.

One of the interesting aspects of the backstory to Puryear's *Big Phrygian* is the fact that, while he knows the various histories associated with it, he doesn't bring any particular narrative into the foreground; doesn't, in fact, make any one of them the point of the work, even in a sculpture pointedly titled *Shackled* (2014). At the same time, "*Moi libre aussi*" ("I am free too"), the caption beneath the eighteenth-century print of a Black man proudly wearing the red cap, reproduced on the announcement card, is equally applicable to the sculptor, Puryear. Through his art, Puryear both asserts and reminds us that he too is free to work (like his white counterparts) in any way that he pleases.

In fact, the declaration "I am free too" serves multiple roles. It claims equality, while remaining true to the individual's historical context. By using this image as his announcement card, Puryear openly challenges mainstream society's belief that an artist of color should become a particular kind of spokesperson for his or her racial or ethnic community, and must speak in a certain way about certain subjects. Most often, the spokesperson that mainstream society praises understandably divides the world into "us and them." Puryear, however, reminds us that the divisions separating everyone into groups and hierarchies are porous and constantly changing.

By not using a reassuring narrative—or the reassurance of narrative itself—to foreground *Big Phrygian* and the related works, Puryear invites viewers to engage with the form itself and all the different ways he has brought it into existence. This is where John Keats comes in. In a letter, dated December 21, 1817, sent to his brothers George and Thomas, John Keats begins formulating the basis of his poetic belief:

> I mean Negative Capability, that is when man is capable of being in uncertainties, Mysteries, doubts, without any irritable reaching after fact & reason."

Not only does Keats spell out the deep, unavoidable conflict between the artist's imagination and his capacity for self-criticism (which has been called doubt), but he also proclaims the necessity to reject "reaching after fact & reason."

Less than a year later, in a letter dated October 27, 1818, sent to his friend Richard Woodhouse, Keats observed:

> What shocks the virtuous philosopher delights the chameleon poet [. . .]. A poet is the most unpoetical of anything in existence, because he has no Identity.

Keat's "chameleon poet" anticipates Charles Baudelaire's "passionate spectator [. . .] who everywhere rejoices in his incognito." An artist or poet, without projecting a fixed identity, exists on the opposite end of the spectrum from the individual who is celebrated for producing signature works.

In our postmodern age, when sampling, copying, branding, deskilling, and lack of creativity are commonplace, and even celebrated, in what has recently been defined as our "atemporality," or our time of timelessness, Keats's belief in "Negative Capability" and the artist's ability to live in "uncertainties" must seem quaint. And yet it was Keats's contribution to theory that came to mind when I was looking at Puryear's work, especially *Big Phrygian*. Looking at and thinking about his work, I realized how often Puryear must have refused to give himself a way out and sought certainty. In contrast to many other sculptors, Puryear has never become formulaic. Since he began exhibiting in 1972, he has remained fresh, even as he broadened his work. By using the Phrygian cap as a starting point, he takes a potent symbol and makes it his own, even as he rejects the obvious markers of subjectivity and the "I." Moreover, he brings history back into sculpture, something that was supposedly banished by the rise of modernist sculpture and the innovative work of Constantin Brancusi.

Knowing that he was going to die from tuberculosis, Keats transcended his stricken state to write poems in which imagination overcame all obstacles without denying their existence. Puryear, a Black artist working during a time of pronouncements of all kinds about what should and should not be done, declares, "I am free too." By doing so, Puryear speaks both for himself and for any artist who refuses to conform to expectations, refuses to become easily identified or reach after the reassurances offered by fact and reason.

This is the undeniable greatness that they share.

NOTES

I.

PLEASE WAIT BY THE COATROOM

1 Césaire, Aimé. *The Collected Poetry*, translated with introduction and notes by Clayton Eshleman and Annette Smith. Berkeley: University of California Press, 1983, 67.

2 Fouchet, Max-Pol. *Wifredo Lam*. Barcelona: Ediciones Poligrafa S. A., 1976, 188-89.

3 Rubin, William S. *Dada, Surrealism, and Their Heritage*. New York: Museum of Modern Art, 2nd Edition, 1977, 171.

4 Maurer, Evan. "Dada and Surrealism" in *"Primitivism" In 20th Century Art: Affinity of the Tribal and the Modern*, Volume II, Edited by William S. Rubin. New York: Museum of Modern Art, 1984, 580.

5 Ibid., 583.

II.

RETHINKING ISAMU NOGUCHI'S GREATNESS

1 Noguchi, Isamu. Oral history interview, Paul Cummings, *Archives for American Art*, November 7-December 26, 1973.

2 Altshuler, Bruce. *Noguchi*. New York: Abbeville Press, 1994, 9.

3 Baudelaire, Charles. "The Painter of Modern Life," translated and edited by Jonathan Mayne in *The Painter of Modern Life and Other Essays*. New York: Phaison Press, second edition, 1995, 9.

4 Altshuler, *Noguchi*, 18.

5 Baudelaire, "The Painter of Modern Life," 7.

6 Gale, Peggy, ed. *Artists Talks 1969–1977*. Nova Scotia, Canada: The Press N.S.C.A.D, 2004, 15–16.

RICHARD HUNT'S INDISPUTABLE ACHIEVEMENT

1 In addition to *Arachne*, MoMA owns a number of Hunt's lithographs printed at Tamarind Lithography Workshop in 1965 and one printed at Lakeside Press in 1969, as well as an unusual copper-resist drawing dated 1979; see https://www.moma.org/collection/works/38243.

2 Lieberman, William S. "Introduction," *The Sculpture of Richard Hunt*. New York: The Museum of Modern Art, 1971, 5.

3 Castro, Jan Garden. "Richard Hunt: Freeing the Human Soul," *Sculpture* 17, no. 5 (May–June 1998), 34–39; available online at https://sculpturemagazine.art/richard-hunt-freeing-the-human-soul/.

4 Glaser, Bruce. Edited by Lucy R. Lippard. "Questions to Stella and Judd," *ARTnews* (September 1966).

5 Yau, John. "Please Wait by The Coatroom," *Arts Magazine* 63, no. 4 (December 1988), 56–59. In the essay, the author points out that William S. Rubin, director of the department of painting and sculpture at MoMA from 1973 to 1988, designated Lam as "the first Surrealist to make primitive and ethnic sources central to his art," depriving him of his birthright.

THE UNSEEN PROFESSORS: ON LEO AMINO, MINORU NIIZUMA, AND JOHN PAI

1 Judd, Donald. "Specific Objects," *Arts Yearbook*, no. 8 (1965).

2 In *The Triumph of American Painting: A History of Abstract Expressionism* (New York: Harper & Row, 1970), Irving devotes a chapter to the eleven artists he feels are central to Abstract Expressionism. None of them are women or artists of color. In his follow-up book about the second generation, *The New York School: The Painters & Sculptors of the Fifties* (1978), Sandler writes about thirty-nine artists, six of whom are women. There are no artists of color.

3 Aconci, Vito. "Leo Amino," *ARTnews* (May 1970), 20.

4 Niizuma, Minoru. "Listening to Stone," interview by Tadayasu Sakai. *Paris: Galerie Nichido*, 1989, n.p.

III.

ON RECONSIDERING IDENTITY IN ART

1 Cabrera, Lydia. *Afro-Cuban Tales*. Lincoln: University of Nebraska Press, 2004.

MING SMITH'S NECESSARY ANGELS

1 Smith, Ming, "A Photographer Who Made 'Ghosts' Visible," interview by Maurice Berger, *The New York Times*, January 11, 2017.

MEETING PLACES: ON SIAH ARMAJANI

1 Heidegger, Martin. "Building Dwelling Thinking," *Poetry, Language, Thought*, translated by Alfred Hofstadter. New York: Harper & Row, 1971, 145–61.

2 Emerson, Ralph Waldo. *The Complete Works*, 1904, Vol. II. *Essays: First Series*, XII, "Art." Online at Bartleby.com.

IV.

ALL THE WORLD'S A STAGE: THE ART OF MARTIN WONG

1 Cameron, Dan. "Brick by Brick: New York According to Martin Wong," *Sweet Oblivion: The Urban Landscpe of Martin Wong*, edited by Dan Cameron and Amy Scholder. New York: New Museum and Rizzoli, 1988, 2. "obsessive-compulsive method," Ibid.

2 Schwabsky, Barry. "A City of Bricks and Ciphers," *Art in America* (September 1998), 100–105.

3 Cameron, "Brick by Brick," 2. Four things strike me about Wong's sartorial preferences. First, he was extremely self-possessed and confident. Second, he liked to challenge stereotypes, particularly when it came to popular culture's view of Chinese Americans. In the winning of the West, the Chinese worked on the railroad and

ran restaurants and laundries. They were not cowboys and not seen as heroic. Third, he wasn't afraid of calling attention to himself, qualities that mainstream society does not associate with a Chinese American male, a member of the model minority. Fourth, Wong was drawn to the theatrical, to costumes.

4 Blinderman, Barry. "The Writing on the Wall," *Sweet Oblivion: The Urban Landscape of Martin Wong*, Exhibition Catalogue (1998), 21.

5 Ibid., "The Writing on the Wall," 18.

6 Ramirez, Yasmin. "La Vida: The Life and Writings of Miguel Piñero in the Art of Martin Wong," in *Sweet Oblivion*, edited by Cameron and Scholder, 35. In recounting the beginning of their friendship, Ramirez writes: "Piñero was an extraordinary performer who could emote both the pathetic and the menacing aspects of the personas he created, and Wong was moved by what he heard. After the opening Wong struck up a conversation with Piñero and, feeling an 'instant affinity' with the poet, invited Piñero to see more of his art. Piñero visited a few days later and they became fast friends. In a matter of weeks, Wong's apartment became a 'hideout' for Piñero and a posse of four young men whom he adopted as apprentices. Pito a.k.a. Little Ivan, Little Brian, and the twins, Peter and Marty." 37.

7 Ibid., 39.

ACKNOWLEDGMENTS

A lot of people helped make this book what it is, starting with the editors and curators who enabled me to write about these subjects, and the colleagues who helped me say it better. The first person I want to thank is Barry Schwabsky, who published "Please wait by the coatroom: Wifredo Lam in the Museum of Modern Art" in *Arts Magazine* in 1988 when no other art magazine would have considered it. That set the ball rolling.

There have been who helped me develop my thoughts, sharpen my writing, and showed me it was possible to see with my own eyes. Their support has been invaluable. I want to acknowledge the importance of Jacob "Jake" Grossberg (1932–2014), John Ashbery (1927–2017), Ted Potter (1933–2006), Paul Cummings (1933–1997), Richard Martin (1947–1999), Ingrid Sischy (1952–2015), Robert "Bob" Lee, Margo Machida, Lowery Stokes Sims, Gabriella Rangel, Lesley King-Hammond, Lou Laurin Lam (1934–2012), Eskil Lam, Luis Jimenez (1940–2006), Karen Higa (1966–2013), Russell Ferguson, Tina Kim, Helen Molesworth, Melissa Rachleff, Jon Ott, Jonathan Laib, Thomas Micchelli, Albert Mobilio, Tammy Nguyen, Natalie Haddad, and Hrag Vartanian in the making of this book.

Many of these essays and reviews have previously appeared in a different form in *Arts Magazine, Hyperallergic,* and in museum and gallery publications.

I want to thank Joshua Bodwell, Celia Johnson, and Elizabeth Blachman at Black Sparrow Press for the care they put into this book.

I also want to thank my family, Eve and Cerise.

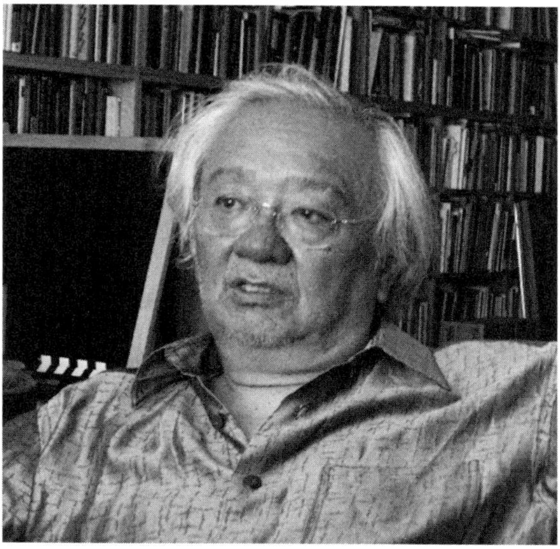

JOHN YAU is a poet, fiction writer, art critic, and curator who began writing about art in 1978, when his reviews first appeared in *Art in America*. Since then, he has contributed essays to more than 200 catalogs and museum publications, curated exhibitions, and been the arts editor for *The Brooklyn Rail* (2007-2011) and regular contributor to the online magazine *Hyperallergic* (since 2012). The author of monographs on Jasper Johns, Liu Xiaodong, Catherine Murphy, A. R. Penck, and many others, he received the Rabkin Prize for art criticism in 2021.

Printed March 2023 in Hanover, Pennsylvania for the Black Sparrow Press by Sheridan. Set in Eames Century Modern with Neue Kabel for display. Interior design by Tammy Ackerman. This first edition has been bound in a jacketed hardcover.

Black Sparrow Press was founded by John and Barbara Martin in 1966 and continued by them until 2002. The iconic sparrow logo was drawn by Barbara Martin.